FROM SIDE TO SIDE

A Walk across England and Wales

JOYCE TOMBS

PRAXIS BOOKS

Praxis Books
"Sheridan", Broomers Hill Lane, Pulborough, West Sussex.
RH20 2DU

Copyright © Joyce Tombs, 1999

The Author asserts her moral right to be recognised as the author of this work.

ISBN 0 9528420 4 1

British Library Cataloguing-in-Publication Data. A catalogue record for this book is available from the British Library.

Printed by Intype Ltd, Wimbledon.

All rights reserved. No part of this publication may be reproduced, stored in a retrieval system, or transmitted in any form or by any means, electronic, mechanical, photocopying, recording or otherwise without the prior permission of the publisher.

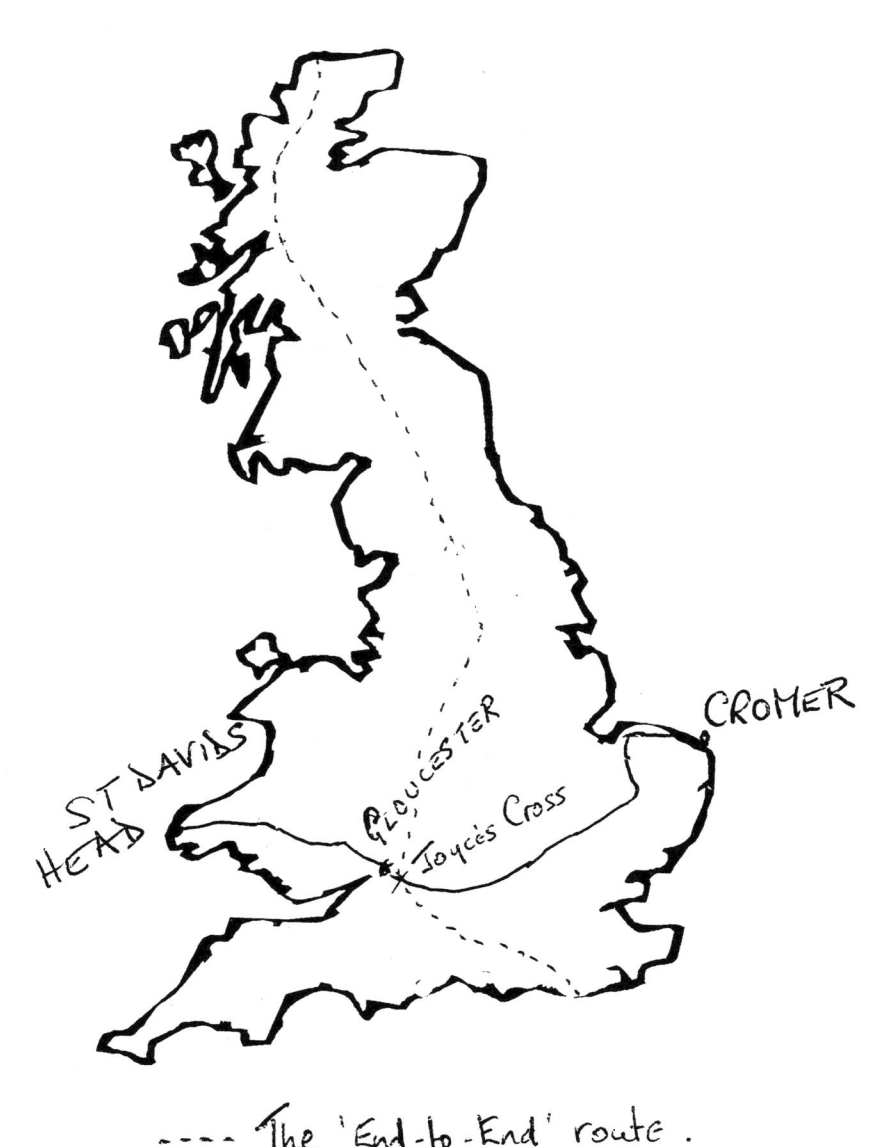

Author's Note: This poem was written for me by Lesley Dunn, who has been a willing and enthusiastic accomplice in numerous projects and to whom, in recognition of her contribution, this book is dedicated.

As you begin your 'Side to Side',
A walk across the country wide,
I wish for you a peaceful start
Along the Norfolk coastal part,
With level ground and bracing air
The strains of winter to repair!
    Each project that we choose to do
    Is self-creation; we renew
    Our selves, our goals; we change, we grow
    We make *new* plans, some seeds we sow.
    So with this thought, I hope you'll find
    Adventures of the joyful kind!
    With hidden 'treasures', views galore
    As ancient trackways you explore.
    On newer paths, surprises sweet
    Both sights and all the folk you meet.
    And if some mishaps you report
    Let's hope they're of the mirthful sort.
    And as you tramp the many miles
    Let's hope you can avoid high stiles!
    And when you want to rest and eat
    I hope you'll find a pleasant seat!
        In England's middle, you will wend
        Your way, to cross your 'End to End',
        The kindred point of both your routes
        (But not, I think, in self-same boots!)
        I wish you great success - and more -
        Your journey to the Western shore
        This year or next, I hope you reach
        St David's land, the Celtic beach.
        To end: I wish you shoals of LUCK
        To match up with your splendid *pluck!*

CONTENTS

	Introduction	8
CHAPTER 1	Folk Like Us	9
CHAPTER 2	Going Slowly	19
CHAPTER 3	East Anglian Spring	31
CHAPTER 4	Adventures of the joyful kind	49
CHAPTER 5	A Turning Point	59
CHAPTER 6	Going, going....	71
CHAPTER 7	Oxfordshire Summer	86
CHAPTER 8	Real walkers	95
CHAPTER 9	All the way to Wales	111
CHAPTER 10	Not the Little Chef	131
CHAPTER 11	On the Roller Coaster	139
CHAPTER 12	One more river...	149
CHAPTER 13	For the Record	165
Bibliography		170
Index		171

Introduction

In 1996, Joyce Tombs published *By Way of Beachy Head*, the story of her 1000-mile walk from the Sussex coast to the northern point of Scotland. At the end of that book, she expressed the intention to balance that walk with another, from the east coast of England to the western extremity of Wales. In 1998, aged almost seventy-five, she accomplished that second ambition.

From Side to Side is a darker story in many ways. If we disliked the traffic and roads in the first book, we utterly detest them now. The infamous A40, subject of great loathing across the land, is an abiding example of England's ruination for walkers. Joyce's sketch maps rarely omit it as a constant presence - until in the final chapters, she forgives it a little, as the road also mellows.

Joyce's discovery that B&Bs cannot always be found in the less scenic areas of England is a frustration and a worry to her. The realisation that only certain parts of the country are assumed to be 'walkable' now is an unwelcome one. The domination of road traffic in many parts of England is a blight we have allowed to creep up on us, and even now we have little idea of the price we have paid for our collective abandonment of walking or cycling as viable means of transport.

The book is another excellent and inspiring read. It is also a valuable snapshot of our country in the late 90s. Once again, we are invited to muse on our own reactions and to think about what we would have done in Joyce's boots. We can dream and plan ways in which we might make our own seventy-fifth year as original and memorable as she did.

Becky Smith. Summer 1999

Chapter 1

Folk Like Us

O long before the bere was steeped for malt
And long before the grape was crushed for wine,
The glory of the march without a halt,
The triumph of a stride like yours and mine
Was known to folk like us who walked about
To be the sprightliest cordial out and out!.

John Davidson

'Mum, can we do the Pennine Way?'

This was our youngest son, Robert, speaking. He must have been twelve, because it was the following year, 1978, when he was thirteen, that he and I set out from Edale and walked the two hundred and seventy miles to Kirk Yetholm. I think you may say it was a formative experience for both of us.

I knew about the Pennine Way, of course - what walker doesn't? But the idea of doing it had been relegated to the 'I wish I could' realm, with Dick, who had been a faithful walking companion throughout the years of our marriage, rather dissociating himself from the notion of this particular long-distance walk. It now dawned on me that with our older children planning their own holidays I could make time and space for myself to do something I'd been hankering after without really knowing it might be possible.

The account of that walk would need at least a chapter to itself, so I'll leave it by saying that the Pennine Way was the first of many long-distance walks. The point of mentioning it here is that one of the many things it taught me was the importance of forward planning. Since it was my last-born I was subjecting to the perils of peat moors and high hills, I felt a particular sense of responsibility. I was therefore careful to book our hostel beds in advance and ensure we were properly prepared by doing training walks. I also spent long hours studying maps and reading. I think I knew Alfred Wainwright's *Pennine Way Companion* by heart.

Advance preparation has thus been part of the process of every long-distance walk I've done since. I don't think I could ever set out without some of this foreknowledge.

I think I am fortunate in my friends and family, because after I returned from walking to Cape Wrath whereas some might ask if I hadn't had enough of going off on long walks, the question was 'What next?' Thus the idea was born of a side-to-side walk across England and Wales. The process of planning began when I wrote in the final chapter of *By Way of Beachy Head:*

> 'Somewhere simmering on the back burner are the ingredients of another long walk; one that would start on the east coast where East Anglia reaches out into the North Sea and finish on one of the Welsh headlands which meet the Irish Sea. By 1998, which will see my seventy-fifth birthday, I should be ready to depart.'

A side-to-side walk seemed an appropriate follow-up to an

end-to-end one, dividing England, Scotland and Wales roughly into quarters. On my earlier walk I had not set foot in Wales, and it seemed wrong not to do so now. The commitment to a future project would give me a focus and having made it I could leave the process on the back burner and get on with my life. That life was contented enough, keeping in touch with a circle of friends and relations including a new grandchild; trying to improve my French and keep fit; having an interest in current affairs and active in pressure and environmental groups; spending walking holidays in Britain and France; and dealing with the minor crises and emergencies attendant upon living in a Victorian house on the fringes of London. I could let time go by secure in the knowledge that, often outside of conscious thought, preparation for another long walk was under way.

In the spring of 1997, it was time to turn the heat up a notch. By then I had gathered together various aids to planning: articles about parts of the route, some maps, a guidebook lent by a friend. I had a sketch-plan of a route, and as I discovered more about it I grew keenly interested in the ancient roads which I would use for much of the first half of the walk, from Cromer to somewhere along the Ridgway. This would be straightforward. After that I would have little in the way of established long-distance paths to follow. I would need to draw a line on the map and keep to that as far as possible.

It was a book by Edward Thomas, *The Icknield Way*, which told me more about ancient trackways and their history, and about some of the questions still to be answered about their origins and destinations. Edward Thomas is best known as a World War One poet but was also a long-distance walker with a profound love of the countryside. He describes a walk along the Icknield Way from Thetford in Norfolk to Wanborough in Wiltshire just before the outbreak of war. The book is written in beautiful and evocative prose, and describes a country much of which is now lost to us; but more than that it gives us Thomas' concept of roads, and a philosophy of the meaning and purpose of roads through the ages.

Thomas wanted to find out where the Icknield Way ended in the west of England or even in Wales and wrote that he 'could find no excuse for supposing it to go to Wales ....and so to St David's which is now as holy as Rome', but 'the utmost reward of [the] conjecturing traveller would be to find himself ....beside the tomb of Giraldus at St David's itself.'

I had no more excuse than Thomas for expecting to find a drove road across Wales, but could at least go and take a look. I had been given a route: along the Icknield Way to White Horse Hill on the Ridgeway, north across the Thames to Lechlade and Cirencester, to cross the Severn river at Gloucester, thence due west across Wales to reach St David's Head in Dewi-land on the Pembrokeshire coast.

I could see that this walk would be different from the one from Beachy Head to Cape Wrath, completed in 1992. Much of it would be along roads, whereas for most of the end-to-end I had been striving to escape from them, using routes which crossed open and sometimes trackless country: the South Downs Way, the Pennine Way and large areas of the

Scottish Highlands. This new walk would actively seek out the most ancient of English and Welsh roads, some still closed to four-wheeled traffic, some to be shared with modern pilgrims using modern forms of transport.

One road which I spent much of the Welsh section trying to avoid - not always successfully - was the A40 trunk road, which joins Central London with the ferryport at Fishguard in West Wales via Oxford, Gloucester, and Monmouth. The A40 has unashamedly usurped routes used by travellers of old, changing them beyond recognition but sometimes leaving no other route for the walker. News of my close encounters with the A40 will be given from time to time in this chronicle.

I first wondered about doing the walk over a two-year period, England in 1998 and Wales in 1999, but the total distance I estimated to be something under five hundred miles, rather less than I had walked from Beachy Head to the Scottish Border in 1991. Barring unforeseen problems I should be able do it in one go. One way or another, plans were taking shape, and my enthusiasm for the walk was growing. Along with this enthusiasm went a kind of grieving for Edward Thomas and all those who did not survive World War One; the freshness of Thomas's prose made me feel very close to him and to others who had walked where I planned to go.

Anyone planning an extended absence from home needs, essentially, sufficient time and space to do it, and this is easy enough if, like me, you have the immense advantage of being no longer tied to work and a young family. You need, too, a supportive spouse who will, without complaint, take on additional housekeeping tasks. Not everyone is so fortunate; John Hillaby in his account of walking across Europe tells of meeting a young man who longed to go on similar travels, and of his sadness in finding that the young man could not go because he owned a travel agency! You need enough money of course, and again I had the good fortune to be financially secure enough to be able to afford the trip. Young people think nothing of leaving home with tent and sleeping bag and little else, and earning some money along the way, but I had reached a stage where I wanted to have a bed to go to of a night-time.

As 1997 went by I did an audit of my preparedness for another long walk. I didn't feel as fit as I was in 1991, when I had spent time in marathon training and in taking part in long-distance challenge walks. I have always prided myself on my stamina, of being able to keep going over time, so would need to draw on this to get me through the first week or so until the business of putting one foot after another had become a matter of routine. I also had an uncomfortable feeling of not being sufficiently prepared in my knowledge of the areas where I proposed to travel and would have to compensate for this as I went along.

Lowestoft is the most easterly point of East Anglia, and thus a logical starting-point for a side-to-side walk. But I chose Cromer in preference as marking the start of the Norfolk coast path. This goes along or near to the shoreline over cliffs, sand-dunes and sea defences, enclosing marshes and mudflats, through a number of small seaside towns and passing bird sanctuaries - North Norfolk being celebrated for its bird life. This would be new territory to me; earlier experience of Norfolk had been in wartime days, when as a WAAF transport driver I had served on bomber stations and never even seen the sea. I was thinking of this first week of walking as an acclimatisation period. 'Norfolk is so bracing' I kept being told.

I would travel really light. I've never been one for taking luxuries like hairdryers or comforts like teddy bears but it's very easy to throw in the odd extra garment, book or radio, and think the difference would not matter. This time would be different. Everything would be chosen on the grounds of a] weight and b] need. So the unbreakable thermos specially bought for me by Dick for my birthday was cast aside as was my walkman radio. Spare clothing was cut to the minimum: one T-shirt and a lightweight jumper, thin cotton leggings, nightie, one spare pair of knickers and one pair of socks, in addition to essential waterproofs. I saved ends of toothpaste tubes and relied on finding soap and towel on overnight stays. I counted on never being too far from shop, doctor or hospital in case of accident or illness, so for a medicine chest I carried only a few aspirins and six plasters. My (obligatory) book would be the one with fewest pages consistent with being worth reading (Evelyn Waugh's *Scoop* as it happened). Maps guidebooks and writing materials were weighty essentials, but I committed the sacrilege of removing the covers from maps and copying relevant parts of guides.

I discovered that I lacked several of the Ordnance Survey Landranger maps which covered the early parts of the walk through East Anglia and rashly thought that I didn't need to carry so many. I decided that, using the Coast Path and Icknield Way Guides, there were some I could manage without. As a fallback I would carry a twenty-year-old Ordnance Survey quarter-inch map of East Anglia, which would, I thought, serve as a supplement to the guides. This proved to be a big mistake.

I checked my gear; my Brasher boots, bought for the End-to-End, still had plenty of life in them, as had my Goretex waterproof. I had a new Lowe Alpine Walkabout rucksack which I was well pleased with, and had invested in a Leki three-section walking stick, which I had been assured did wonders for knees. My final purchase was of a Peter Storm fleece jacket to protect me against the rigours of the East Anglian spring.

I had set my date of departure as April 18th, the Saturday after Easter Monday 1998, with the hope of arriving at St David's Head on June 21st, the summer solstice. This should allow plenty of time for rest days and I needn't hurry, I thought. My rucksack, when packed, weighed between twelve and thirteen pounds. I was wearing my Ron Hills trousers, my green cotton/polyester walking shirt over a T-shirt, said Brasher boots and new Bridgedale socks, fleece jacket, and my cherished tweed hat. My knees were protected by Tubigrip supports, as was my still weak ankle. I had booked bed and breakfasts three nights ahead, and was ready to go.

Many people have reason to remember the Easter weekend of 1998. It had been an early spring; in our garden snowdrops, crocuses and daffodils were blooming at the same time in mid-February. But mid-April saw the onset of the cold spell known to country-dwellers as the 'blackthorn winter'. Heavy and persistent rain caused serious flooding in the Midlands and East Anglia; our television screens had been full of the news of blocked roads, flooded rivers, loss of life. Flood alerts were still in operation in East Anglia. It was still raining. It didn't seem the most favourable time to start a long walk. And - I'm almost ashamed to admit this - I wasn't well, having picked up a virus of some kind a week earlier. I had a nasty cough which kept me awake at night and a slightly raised temperature and felt that the last thing I wanted to do was to start on a walk of nearly five hundred miles.

But, of course, I did decide to go because by that time staying at home was equally out of the question.

The account which follows is of a walk which can in no way be described as arduous. I don't like to plead advancing age as an excuse, but realistically I can no longer contemplate walking for twenty miles a day for several successive days; twelve miles a day is a good average and fifteen is rather too much. I find it difficult to carry a pack over rough ground, so I ruled out, for example, crossing the Brecon Beacons in Wales, although those hills would have been on my direct route. I did, however, encounter unexpected obstacles in the way of finding accommodation, coping with weather, and, overwhelmingly, coping with the feeling of being an intruder in an environment where the motor-car had come increasingly to rule, and this leads me to conclude that a long-distance walk can never be easy. Any problems are simply different for different people.

April 18th inevitably came, and Dick walked with me to our local station, I suspected secretly alarmed at the snail-like pace which was all that I could manage. I was trying hard not to show how miserably ill I was feeling. It was a relief when I was able to board the train. Dick had offered me the crossword page of the *Financial Times*, as I refused to buy a weighty Saturday paper; and all that was missing were the down clues, which misguidedly I had torn out to save weight!

Chapter 2

Going Slowly

With level ground and bracing air
The strains of winter to repair
Lesley Dunn

When I alighted from the branch line train at Cromer it was still raining. The only cover where I could shelter to put on my Goretex jacket was a squalid bus-shelter-like hovel with a pile of sweet and fish-and-chip wrappers in the corner. The station was elevated and down some steps opposite the platform was a large car park outside - yes, of course - a large Safeway supermarket. Was this, I wondered, what I had left home for?

I was approaching the next few days as a prologue, a brief interlude before the 'real' part of the walk was to begin. This was rather unfair to the Norfolk coast, which has charms of its own, but at the time I didn't know that, and I think I was more interested in survival.

The coast path guide leads the walker inland from Cromer to meet the sea further along the coast, at West Runton. On the basis that a coast-to-coast walk should actually begin on the seashore, preferably at a point where one might at least dip a toe in the water, I headed for where I thought the coast would be. There weren't many people about, most of them hurrying to escape the blustery wind. I crossed a main road and came to a cliff top to find the sea below it invisible in the

Cromer to Thornham.

mixture of drizzle and wind-driven spume. I decided a scramble down a cliff wasn't on my itinerary, but at least there was a footpath heading in the direction of Sheringham, a mere five miles distant and my destination for the night.

The footpath soon came up against a high barrier guarding a caravan site. Past this was another footpath, then another caravan site, and so on. I went on slowly, having to stop from time to time just to get my breath. I came to the outskirts of Sheringham and found myself on its seafront, rather a nice one guarded by a hill with a large building on top and a view along the cliffs. By now the rain had stopped and a chill wind was blowing. I joined a population of warmly-clad seaside visitors parading the main street, which contained the mixture of souvenir shops and eating places habitually found in seaside towns. I found the Copper Kettle cafe and warmed up over Earl Grey tea and a toasted teacake.

Olivedale, my B&B was just around the corner from the High Street, my room on the second floor of a seaside boarding house, which, like numbers of establishments I was to use, proclaimed its no-smoking rule. It seemed a long way up two flights of stairs but the room was warm and the bathwater hot and after a while I felt sufficiently restored to return to the High Street to eat at one of the many fish restaurants. I wasn't really feeling any better but at least I'd started and was recognising the old feeling of having entered a different dimension where all the preoccupations of one's 'normal' daily life had melted away. I wrote in my diary 'I still feel pretty ill, but, to coin a phrase, things can only get better.'

Next morning I asked for a poached egg for brek and a bacon sandwich to take away and, determined this time to reach the sea, found my way on to a shingle beach, soon to reach a lifeboat station below an impassable cliff. I retreated to the cliff-top again, and found a fingerpost which pointed to the Coast Path past the paddling pool and led to the golf course. 'Be wary of the cliffs and golfers' said the guide. So I was wary, keeping an eye open for stray golf balls, and treading carefully around those places where the encroaching sea had taken huge bites out of the cliff. In this tree-less area there weren't many signs of spring, only a few daisies and dandelions in bloom, but it was fine, the early mist was clearing, and a skylark was singing. I came to a hilltop and looked back at the houses of Sheringham. Inland, a steam train was puffing along, the Bluebell Line of the North Norfolk Railway which runs between Sheringham and Weybourne. This was a fine walk, on short turf along the crumbling cliffs but I wondered how long the golf course had to go before it, too, followed the sizeable acres of East Anglia washed away by the sea. I came to a coastguard house and left the cliff to walk into Weybourne past a windmill, hoping to find somewhere for coffee. But the pubs looked dauntingly full of Sunday lunchers and before I knew it I was through the village and following the main road towards Cley, looking for another way to the coast path.

I climbed a steep hill (unexpected where I had thought to be upon level ground) and came to the entrance to the Muckleburgh Museum which houses a large collection of World War Two armoured vehicles, tanks and the like. Opposite was a friendly seat which bore a dedication in honour of the Silver Jubilee of George Fifth 1935. Feeling drained and offering thanks to the good burghers of Norfolk for their provision of seats I stretched out for an extended siesta and lunch, actually feeling warmth in the sun.

Salthouse, which came next, was jolly, with an ice-cream van and children feeding the waterfowl. People armed with binoculars and cameras were walking purposefully along a footpath directing them to the Cley bird sanctuary. I walked along the road dodging too much traffic and found another hill to climb to take me over and down into Cley, round the backs of old flint cottages and gardens with spring flowers. I joined the road with, of course, a view of the famous windmill and walked along the little cobbled main street to find my B&B in Marshland House.

Next day took me on to the salt marshes near Blakeney, a wild lonely expanse of coarse grass and muddy inlets, with the long finger of Blakeney Point reaching out seawards into the haze. After the harbour and gardens of the houses along Morston Quay I was alone except for the seabirds, feeling unnerved by the solitude, in a place which seemed to demand sunshine and family parties rather than this harsh bleakness.

I followed the crest of some low dunes which fell away on to flat muddy wasteland where I had to skirt deep puddles left by high tide and my boots came in for a wetting. 'It is easy to lose your way and be cut off by a rising tide,' said the guide. I came eventually to a deep inlet and a small marina and sat on an upturned boat for a breather. In the distance, on a sandback, I saw what must have been the shapes of basking seals.

The track turned away from the shoreline and crossed a bridge over the inlet. I reached for my guidebook and found I must have left it at my last stop so retraced my steps a half-mile to retrieve it. I should have continued along the coast but the skies were darkening and I heard a rumble of thunder, so instead I climbed a stile and took a signed path heading for the village of Stiffkey. By now it was well past lunchtime and I was wanting food, drink, and most of all a rest, and was wondering what could have persuaded me to come on this walk.

The path was all right as far as it went, over three more stiles to the coast road, then along another little path beside it, which eventually petered out leaving me with the best part of an uphill mile to walk along the road to the village. I reached the first houses and found a seat but the downpour put an early finish to my rest. Stiffkey, like Weybourne, seemed to lack anything in the way of shelter or provision for the weary traveller; even the post office was firmly shut, and there was no sign of a pub. I had four miles to walk to Wells-next-the Sea where I was to spend the night.

This was, of course, the third day of my walk, and I should have remembered that it was inevitable that at some point in the early stages I would feel like giving up before I had a sufficient number of miles under my boots to make it seem worthwhile to continue. I set out along the coast road where the landscape was flat and uninteresting, and I rather grudged every step that I took. When an elderly gentleman driving a smart new Mercedes stopped and offered me a lift ('You look tired,' he said) I didn't really think twice about whether this was cheating or a signal to abandon the whole enterprise. I just said weakly 'I know I shouldn't.....' and slung my rucksack on the rear seat, dripping all over the immaculate upholstery. Within ten minutes I was getting out of the car outside Cobbler's which was to be my night's lodging.

Paradoxically, cheating like this had the effect of restoring my morale; I felt I had given myself permission to make the walk easier for myself, and I sat drinking tea in the comfortable conservatory feeling that the world was treating me better than I deserved. I was keeping to the schedule I had set myself, and in two days would be leaving the coast path to join the Peddar's Way.

This optimism continued as I walked next day on to the harbour front. Wells is the only port left on the North Norfolk coast with a useable harbour but in my book and despite its name, Wells isn't really next the sea. There's a mile to walk on the sea bank alongside a long inlet to where a flight of steps leads on to the beach. Where the access road ends was an oversize camping and caravan site, largely unoccupied today, with sand-dunes planted with pine trees screening it from the beach. I climbed the steps to have a look at the seashore (sand and groynes) and coming down just missed an encounter with the only other backpacker I was to see on the coast path. He was coming through the gate from the lakeside track below. I had begun to doubt whether other foot-travellers like myself still existed in a setting where everybody else - bird-watchers, tourists, walkers, residents - seemed dependent on car transport.

I left Wells behind to follow the sandy track through pine woods, easy walking with the sea murmuring beyond the dunes. I reached a well-occupied car park and turned away from the sea on to the long Lady Anne's Drive which took me back on to the coast road and to the gates of Holkham Hall, one of the stately homes with which North Norfolk abounds. The Holkham estate is noted for its association with Thomas Coke who in the eighteenth century revolutionised English agriculture, turning thousands of acres of barren heathland into fertile farming country, and thus transforming North Norfolk's landscape. I diverged from the coastal path to enter the well-cared for grounds of Holkham Hall which was shut until the end of the month, but my spies had informed me that there was a tea-shop, which I managed to find just a few minutes before it closed for lunch. I had coffee and cake in the company of many well-dressed car travellers.

Holkham Beach has sand as far as the eye can see. I followed a meandering course looking for firm patches, then trudged along the sea bank to meet the road at Burnham Overy Staithe, with a fine little harbour but no post office or shop. I walked back along the road past the pub which was called The Hero, which I marked as a place to eat supper, to find the Domville Guest House tucked away down quiet Glebe Lane.

Long experience of using bed and breakfast has led me to the conclusion that there are two broad categories of provider. Category one is where you are welcomed, shown your room, asked what time you'd like breakfast, and then, short of emergencies like fire or flood, are unlikely to see your host/ess before morning. Category two is where you will be offered tea and usually have the company of your host/ess while you drink it, and there is genuine interest in you as a person rather than as an over-night bringer-in of income. Ann Smith definitely fell into category two, coming to talk and tell me about her childhood home just a few streets away from mine in Sydenham and which she had left to be near family in Norfolk. Ann was the first of many Smiths I was to meet along the way all of whom have been remembered for differing reasons.

This was a favoured stop for bird-watchers, I discovered, finding in the sitting-room logbooks which listed dates and details of birds spotted by different visitors - literally hundreds of them. I felt ashamed of my poor bird-identification abilities, having to confess that I hadn't even spotted the avocets near Burnham beach. My fellow guests, a couple from Norwich, made up for my ignorance in having an impressive list of sightings that day, all carefully recorded. The three of us ended the day in the bar of The Hero, where the food was at best indifferent, and we needed torches for the walk back in the total absence of streetlights.

I discovered my mistake in not having the Ordnance Survey Landranger map with me when I tried next day to find a short cut to Burnham Norton, but after crossing stiles and fields with growing crops I was foiled by a deep dyke without a bridge. My quarter-inch map was of little use here, and I had to retrace my steps and continue by road, which was in fact quite pleasant, with one of the ubiquitous windmills to look at, traffic-free and with long views inland. At Burnham Deepdale I recovered the coast path which went along the backs of houses and past mussel sheds then into National Trust property and past the site of the Roman fort Branodunum. Narrow board walks had been installed here to cross the soggy ground, in places awash and not encouraging me to stray from it, but rather uncomfortable walking. You had to concentrate to avoid putting a boot in. The view offshore was of miles of salt marsh with just a hint of sea in the far distance.

The path rejoined the road at Brancaster, where The Ship pub was open. It had turned warm for the first time this week, so I went in and had shandy and a tuna baguette. From here the guide directed me inland, there being no route on the seaward side of the road to my next objective, Thornham. I chose instead to walk along the road, finding it busier than I expected; school turning out time of course.

I walked along Thornham village street and found a sign directing me down a quiet lane to my destination. Orchard House was set four-square in two acres of garden, with a bird-table and an enclosure for a rabbit, and blissfully secluded. The daffodils were out, three weeks later than at home, but the hedgerows were turning green and a clematis montana was coming into bloom. In the porch was an envelope with my name on it giving instructions about gaining admission to the house in Mrs Rutland's absence, which I managed to follow successfully. I had just made tea when Dick appeared from London, via King's Lynn and a walk along the coast path from Hunstanton. He was to walk with me for the next three days.

When later in the day I met Mrs Rutland she reminded me that we had seen each other the previous evening in The Hero at Burnham. Mrs Rutland was scathing about the standard of cooking there and I remembered that I hadn't enjoyed my ham and chips. So we inspected the dining arrangements at The King's Head carefully before deciding to eat there. I chose dressed crab, feeling that I couldn't leave the Norfolk coast without sampling this regional dish while Dick played safer, choosing haddock.

Any long-distance walker worth the name will have a keen interest in where the next meal is coming from, and so far I had found the villages of the coast path well supplied with eating places: pubs, restaurants or fish and chip shops, providing plenty of choice for evening meals. Because of my insistence on travelling light I wasn't carrying much in the way of iron rations, but found a banana a great stand-by for a mid-morning snack; one of the best energy-giving foods, high in carbohydrate and containing essential minerals.

Thornham was the place where I was to leave the Norfolk coast path to join the Peddar's Way. This part of the walk seemed to have gone too quickly. I felt I should have taken more time to appreciate all the things that were special about the area: the many fine old buildings; the varied coastline, much of it wild and deserted; an awareness of a huge sky and acres of open land; the villages where I had been treated with kindness and hospitality on my five overnight stays; and of course the bird population for which North Norfolk is renowned. Much of the time I felt I was merely surviving. The walk nevertheless, seemed to have done its work in improving my state of health; my cough had almost gone, I was sleeping and eating well and finding that I was less tired after a day's walking. Physical fitness isn't something that happens all at once, it's only gradually that you realise that you don't get out of breath walking uphill any more, and I seemed to have reached that state.

Thornham
Great Bircham
Castle Acre
North Pickenham
Thompson
Stonebridge
THETFORD
Barnham

NORFOLK

Thornham to Barnham.

Chapter 3

East Anglian Spring

For winter's rains and ruins are over.....
And in green underwood and cover
Blossom by blossom the spring begins.
                                    Swinburne

We were wakened at seven by a thunderstorm and heavy rain, soon to be followed by blue skies. Breakfast was fruit and cereal and a bacon sandwich to take away for my second brek. We laid in food supplies in the village, which had been a good stage halt, with its two pubs, stores, and a baker's shop, then left the coast road straight away and began to climb - a long ascent. The sea remained in view for a long time; I looked back waiting for it to disappear and realised that the next coastline I would see would be that of West Wales, some four hundred miles distant.

The walk up to this point had felt very much like a prologue, and in my mind the 'real' part of my walk was just beginning. The Peddar's Way, which would take me to Thetford, was almost certainly developed in its present form by the Romans but is probably pre-Roman in origin. The Way is associated with the insurrections of the Iceni led by Queen Boudicca and would have contributed to her downfall by making East Anglia accessible to Roman troop movements. The route originally may have run from Colchester in Essex to Lincolnshire with a ferry over the

Wash, and would have made links with the major Roman road network throughout England. After the departure of the Romans the Peddar's Way was used as a trading route and drove road. Right up to the middle of the eighteenth century Norfolk's prosperity was derived from sheep, wool and weaving. Nowadays of course, Norfolk is the principal agribusiness farming county of England.

The Peddar's Way is a waymarked national long-distance trail approved by the Countryside Commission. Ninety-four miles in length, it stretches between the Norfolk coast at Holme-next-the-sea and Knettishall Heath near Thetford where it has links with the Icknield Way path. It is possible to walk by long-distance footpath from Cromer on the Norfolk coast to Overton Hill near Avebury in Wiltshire and in so doing to follow in the footsteps of travellers, drovers and pilgrims through the ages from Neolithic times to the present day. These travellers have left traces of their passing throughout. Their cultivation of land helped to shape the countryside we see today, and the tracks they used still permit of free passage over many miles, very often away from towns and cities. It was for me part of the excitement of walking these ancient ways to know that I was seeing some of the same sights as did our ancestors, even though so much of their heritage has been debased by twentieth century human technology.

That day was for finding the Way, a few miles inland from where we left Thornham. We were into the agricultural land of north Norfolk, large unfenced fields with growing crops. The minor road we were on took us over a hill and on to a wooded ridge where we found a footpath leading to farm tracks and thence to a muddy track showing one of the Peddar's Way waymarks. There were more signs of spring here, with primroses and the occasional violet by the wayside and brilliantly flowering cherry trees lined the track. Somewhere in the distance a cuckoo called; had it made a mistake in arriving from Africa so early, we wondered? With the wind blowing from the north there was still a chill in the air, and we had to search for a sheltered spot to stop for our coffee break, using my disowned unbreakable thermos which Dick had taken care to bring along with him.

We left the Peddar's Way to walk off-route into Sedgeford, and a lunch-stop at the King William IV pub. Sedgeford had been our destination for the night, but we had made good time and it was too early to stop so we did some telephoning and continued for another five miles to Great Bircham. This is accessible countryside, with many ungated tracks but we noted that some of these had been obstructed by old farm machinery although still usable by walkers. We deduced that this was to deter owners of four-wheel drive vehicles from using the tracks for recreation.

My concept of Norfolk as being flat was rapidly dispelled. We climbed a long hill expecting at any moment to see the windmill of Great Bircham. This is one of a few remaining working windmills and a famous local sight. It started to rain; we tried to ignore it for a while then realised it was setting in and stopped in the shelter of a wood to put on waterproofs.

As we approached the village I had one of those nagging suspicions telling me that something was wrong, and to my dismay found that somewhere along the road I had lost my Peddar's Way Guide. This was unfortunate; not only did the guide contain our only large-scale maps, but it was on loan to me, and the lender's copious notes in it had made it a rich source of information. I was beginning to feel that I could not be trusted with possessions, since in the six days since leaving London I had left a trail across Norfolk of: a sweater, my book, *Scoop*, a comb, and now this. (There would be more later.) Perhaps my determination to travel light had seeped into my unconscious! And it was still raining.

We found the King's Head, where we had booked earlier in the day, only to discover it securely shut up and no way in. Disinclined to wait around getting wetter we noticed that Country Stores across the road was offering bed and breakfast accommodation and without more ado booked ourselves in there.

We returned to contemplating life without the guidebook. We have long experience of losses on the way, one of the hazards of long-distance walking. If things are left behind you move inexorably away from them, and they are gone for ever. There was a famous occasion in France in the Cevennes when one late evening Dick climbed back up the best part of a mountain to search for a lost camera and didn't find it, while I waited by the roadside wondering if I would ever see him again! The consequence of all this was a long walk in the dark to the nearest town, where we had the utmost difficulty in securing accommodation, a further futile search next day, interviews with various bureaucrats, and, of course, an insurance claim.

We had obviously learned nothing from this experience, since we decided that Dick, being the healthier and faster, should return along our route to the Peddar's Way waymark where we knew we had last handled the guide. This he did, returning hot and without the book an hour later, at least having been able to hitch a lift back. We would have to make do with the quarter-inch map for the next two stages. What is most frustrating about such losses is not knowing the fate of the missing object, whether it is in good hands or just abandoned somewhere to decay, and this loss was particularly baffling. On a minor road where we had seen no walkers or cyclists and almost no motor vehicles, who, seeing a small book, could have picked it up? We would never know.

We consoled ourselves with supper at the King's Head where we were the only guests even though the Italian chef was said to be celebrated. Next morning was preoccupied with finding our way back to the Peddar's Way along minor roads which took us past the extensive woodlands and parklands of Houghton estate and Houghton Hall, built for prime minister Robert Walpole in the eighteenth century. Everything about Norfolk seems large: the houses, the estates, the fields, the sky, even the pigs in the pig farms. A map-reading error took us past the gates of Houghton Hall and into Houghton village, which predictably was well-cared for, with immaculate eighteenth-century houses, built, I learned, to rehouse villagers from Walpole's estate and so preserve his view across the park. We came to crossroads at Harpley which we should also have avoided and as we were consulting the map a motorist pulled up beside us and said 'Are you lost?'

This question has a way of raising my hackles, and I answered firmly, 'Walkers are never lost.' (Implying as against motorists who are. I wasn't telling the truth, of course.) Unconvinced by my reply however, he continued with 'The Peddar's Way is just along the road there.' We ignored his words and went the way we'd been intending to, straight ahead and into Harpley village, which had a shop, something we were to learn was becoming rare in this countryside.

We came to the Peddar's Way eventually, through Little Massingham, just as it started to rain again. This was the beginning of a great tract of open country through which the Peddar's Way is one of the few thoroughfares away from the main road. The Way was just as I'd imagined - an unfenced track between fields, some bare, some green with cereal crops, unpopulated, not even a farm building in sight. This was high country, too, not mountain high, but raised enough above sea level to give that impression of endless space which is so characteristic of parts of East Anglia. A mile along the track there were caravans, not the horse-drawn but the motor kind, a horse with a foal which can't have been more than a few days old, and a hand-written notice asking us to respect the countryside.

The track came into woodland and became a tarmac road. Needing to stop for lunch, the only seating we could find was a straw bale beside a dungheap, my protests against such a cheerless (and smelly) spot being disregarded. Said Dick 'We won't find anywhere else,' taking off his rucksack determinedly. It was a short halt in the cold, with the rain starting again.

The Peddar's Way reaches Castle Acre along two and a half miles of the same Roman road, which the local authority has covered over with tarmac. We shared it with drivers on the school run, which I had come to recognise as a daily event disturbing the rural peace. Castle Acre was a pleasant surprise, for which I would have been prepared had I done adequate reading before the walk. We came into a perfect village square surrounded by old houses and dominated by its ancient gateway. At the far side was the twelfth-century church of Great St James with, I was intrigued to see, a pilgrim scallop shell on its noticeboard, Castle Acre being on a famous pilgrim trail from Ely to Walsingham.

Castle Acre was full of surprises. There were the attractions of the castle, the ruins of the Clunian Priory, and the Ostrich pub, equally venerable, with a wonderful vaulted ceiling above its dining area, and imaginative dishes on its menu. Sadly, I was rather off my food. 'It was the crab,' asserted Dick. 'I said it was a mistake'.

Morning brought more rain. Dick was leaving on his homeward journey and I was looking for somewhere to pass another night, having spent the previous one coping with the crab's aftermath. We walked across the square and found 3 Stocks Green. The door was opened by a woman we later found to be Val Guinness, who greeted us warmly and invited us in to what seemed to be at first glance an incredibly chaotic room. It was large, looking on to the village green, and with a rear window giving a view on to a garden with a yew tree. It was full of sofas and armchairs and littered with video and tape cassettes, books, and at least three chess sets with games in various stages of completion. Talking non-stop Val informed us that the house belonged to her son Rupert who was in town with his market stall, but I could spend the day there and she would give me the key. Moreover, on learning that Dick needed to get to King's Lynn to catch his train, Val immediately responded: 'But I'll drive you there.'

So that is what happened. Dick left with Val, and I spent the best part of the day drowsing in a room which no longer seemed chaotic, but friendly and welcoming. In the afternoon the sun came out and, feeling better, I walked around a village which had now become busy with day visitors and a wedding reception. Rupert arrived, a friendly young man walking with a limp, the result, I learned, of a bad car accident in boyhood. He and his mother, who arrived later, were incredibly kind in a disorganised sort of way, giving me food and drink and, next morning, offering to drive me to Thetford against my protestations that I had to walk there.

Alone with Val over breakfast I learned more about Rupert's horrific accident. He with his father, older brother Peter and another passenger had been involved in a head-on collision while driving back from the airport. The brother and passenger had been killed, and Rupert so badly injured that he was at first not expected to survive. Rupert's recovery, had been slow and difficult, and had left him with some impaired memory although, as I had observed, at the age of twenty-four he was a sensitive and intelligent young man with a keen interest in chess. The family, obviously well-to-do, had been left to cope with all the consequences of the accident which must have irrevocably changed their lives; an unforeseeable event of a kind to which we all at one time or another are vulnerable. I think I left walking more carefully.

Val was an authority on the history of Castle Acre. Number 3 Stocks Green was the oldest house in the village, probably occupied in the eleventh century when the priory was built on land allocated to William de Warenne by his father William the Conqueror. Castle Acre itself has even older associations, having been occupied successively by Britons, Saxons and Romans, before the Norman invasion, which made its later mark on much of Norfolk; vast tracts of land were gifted to his barons by William the Conqueror, in an attempt to stifle dissent.

On a now fine morning I was waved off by Val and Rupert to follow the Peddar's Way past the church and priory and over the gently flowing River Nar to South Acre. Just past Grange Farm I had an encounter with three real Peddar's Way walkers, before meeting groups of young people on a sponsored walk who said I was 'going the wrong way'. On the contrary I was now on the right Landranger map so routefinding had ceased to be a problem for now. Despite yesterday's setback I felt well and optimistic.

I came to the A47 trunk road, one of the few main arteries connecting Norwich with Middle England. One of the charms of Norfolk is the absence of too many main roads. I resisted the temptation to visit the McDonald's which graced the roadside just past a roundabout turbulent with Sunday traffic and waited for an opportunity to cross the road into safer and more tranquil territory.

Once I was back on the track the traffic noise soon became inaudible. I walked between hedges with the hawthorn just coming into bloom and the track becoming increasingly muddy. An unexpectedly strong gust of wind made me dive for the shelter of an oak tree as a clap of thunder was followed by a deluge. The zip fastener of my waterproof jammed as I struggled to put it on, so all in all I was pretty wet by the time the rain eased and I thought it safe to move from the shelter of the tree. Nowhere to sit, of course - there seems to be a dearth of resting places on the Peddar's Way.

Fortunately it was only a short walk into North Pickenham where the Blue Lion was open and I was able to warm up over coffee. The rain stopped and I walked round the village, failing to gain access to the church or even the churchyard, the gate being securely locked.

Norfolk villages seem to like sharing names; besides Great and Little Massingham I had found South and West Acres alongside Castle Acre, and after North I would reach South Pickenham the next day. Next would come Great then Little Cressingham. I wondered how the relative name-places were determined? Surely it can't have been merely a question of size; none of these villages really merited the description 'Great'.

My B&B - Riverside House - was down a little lane near the pub. I went by the house and started to walk up the lane to occupy some time because I thought I was too early, but Mr Norris spied me from the garden and came out into the road to call me back. The house, built in flint like so many in this part of Norfolk, reached down to the River Wissey where there was a footbridge leading to the Norris's garden, two acres of woodland and cultivated land. We sat in the sun and drank tea, and I learned that my hosts were incomers from South London. They told me of floods which they had learned to cope with by sandbagging the front porch. The river had risen to the front door at Easter but had just escaped invading the house. Today a pair of mallards were sailing down a peacefully gurgling stream; it was possible to fish for trout there, said Mr Norris.

Two other guests arrived later, school inspectors come to 'do the Ofsted' on the local primary school, and we sat in the lounge drinking wine and watching the sunset.

The Peddar's Way had been redirected in North Pickenham, prettily, through fields but with the inevitable stiles. I should say here that I have an aversion to stiles, many of which are too high or too rickety for my precarious sense of balance, but these were newly built and easy enough. I crossed the river over a newly-built footbridge and came to the road, which I would be following for four miles to Little Cressingham, modern road-users having adopted the Peddar's Way. Not far from here are the deserted remains of the medieval village of Houghton-on-the-Hill. The eleventh century church of St Mary's which once stood in the centre of the village and was used as a place of worship for many centuries was finally abandoned only earlier this century but has recently been repaired and restored.

I walked on to Little Cressingham, to reach the Red Lion at the crossroads. The bar was occupied by a young woman talking about community care with a young male schoolteacher, notably about drug problems even in this wholly rural community. I turned into a Pilgrim's Way, another route to Walsingham. The way followed the course of a busy B road, but a footpath had been made behind the hedge across fields and took me away from traffic to the Peddar's Way turning. I was coming into Breckland, originally an area of sandy heathland, but now largely afforested, and, sadly, with many acres under army occupation. The Peddar's Way is one of the few routes available for civilian foot traffic, the map copiously adorned with red-lettered 'danger area' signs, some alarmingly adjacent to the Peddar's Way. Fighter planes from the air base at Lakenheath also train over the Thetford forest, so a walk along the Peddar's Way can scarcely be described as peaceful!

I left the Peddar's Way to walk to Pockthorpe Corner and Thatched House, which was what it says it is, a rambling four-hundred-years-old house with all sorts of added extensions, dogs, and a farmer husband. A guest who was staying on holiday had two small dogs of her own, which were kept firmly shut up in her room, their plaintive whimpering heard at intervals. Another guest was, surprisingly, a weekday commuter, working with a solicitor's practice in Thetford and returning home to Cheltenham at weekends. I was to meet others with the same lifestyle in future days.

I'd been expecting at Thatched House to be able to fix up next night's lodging at Thetford, but was offered a rather depressing opinion that 'Thetford was an awful place', having a notorious estate housing a London overspill population. Not at all what the guidebook said about this immemorial city, one of the oldest in England. I made a couple of unproductive telephone calls and left not knowing where I would lay my head that night.

Once rejoined, the Way led through woodland passing the large expanse of the wildlife preserve Thompson water behind its secure fences. Today both Army and Airforce were busy; the rattle of small arms fire was punctuated by the occasional thud of heavy artillery, while overhead there was the screaming of jet fighters. I was looking out for the sooty-faced fatigue-clad trainee combatants I'd been told were to be seen lurking in ditches in these parts and was rather disappointed to find none in evidence.

I planned to leave the Peddar's Way at Stonebridge and walk into Thetford where I was to meet my friend and walking companion Lesley in two days' time. I had hoped to use one of the many forest tracks marked on the map but the Army had commandeered these too; all side turnings bore 'Danger, Keep Out' warnings. It meant an eight-mile road walk.

I came to the Dog and Partridge at Stonebridge and was served with coffee by the landlady, who talked about the decline of village life. There is now no shop or post-office in Stonebridge, and the only bus service a weekly mini-bus organised by the parish council. Pensions are paid out at the pub, a service volunteered by the pub owner.

The sounds of battle accompanied me for most of the way into Thetford, along deserted minor roads, past a huge army camp and along a high heathland hilltop through ranks of pine trees. It was here that another thunderstorm blew up out of the blue, alarming in its intensity but lasting only fifteen minutes. I had throughout the day been attempting to book accommodation in Thetford, using up my dwindling supply of twenty-pence pieces, and was becoming dismayed at my lack of success.

Thetford lived up to its reported reputation in my approach, across the A11 which by-passes the town, then through a characterless housing estate busy with the school rush-hour, groups of secondary school children crowding the pavements. I was feeling desperately tired by now and the way into town seemed endless. I had a list of addresses published by the Icknield Way Association, but at the first I found that the place had changed hands long ago, and at the next learned that all the accommodation was being used by building workers. I called in a small hotel, which was full, but the helpful receptionist directed me along the road towards the station, where, she said, there were two hotels. 'Don't bother to try The Bell,' she warned me. I found a room at the Thomas Paine, which was expensive, but I wasn't going to do any better.

I went through a low patch at Thetford. There seemed so few friendly faces; people seemed to be totally preoccupied with their own affairs and to have little time to spare for the troubles of a lone traveller; I had met no walkers since crossing the A47 near Castle Acre so felt as if I was an odd sort of stranger, an alien from another planet. Accommodation was becoming a real problem. I don't think I had ever before felt that because of not finding somewhere to stay I would be forced to abandon a walk, but at that point it seemed a real possibility. In two days I would be meeting Lesley at Barnham on the Icknield Way but I had still to find somewhere to stay for the morrow.

In the small hours it occurred to me that the train fare to London would be less than the cost of another night at the Thomas Paine. So I caught the early train to King's Cross and was home before lunchtime, giving me time to do my washing, catch up with my three-year-old grandson Jamie whom I had sorely missed and do yet more telephoning in the perennial quest for B&B.

Thetford was better on second acquaintance. It has its attractions in old flint-built buildings and was a major centre for both the Iceni and the Romans for whom it was on the main road across Norfolk. I walked around town, inspected the Ancient House where there is a museum, and paid my respects to Thomas Paine, author of *The Rights of Man* who was born here in 1737 and whose statue stands near the river.

Scenically the way out of Thetford was a vast improvement on the way in. From the town centre and an old bridge a walkway led across parkland with the River Little Ouse adjoining; there was an old mill and an Icknield Way path sign on the ancient Nun's Bridge. Too soon I was back on the main Bury St Edmund's road, but there was a wide grassy verge where I could keep out of the way of the many heavy goods lorries.

Before long I had turned off into the village of Barnham, tucked away out of earshot of traffic noise, but with no shop; with the nearest pub a mile away finding something to eat was going to be a problem.

There's a convention in the B&B world that you wait for an evening meal to be offered, because so few people do now provide it and you don't embarrass them by asking. So I rather diffidently asked if Mrs Head would cook breakfast for me this evening since I didn't eat a cooked breakfast, and was relieved when she agreed. East Farm was a handsome house a hundred and fifty years old, the large rooms beautifully furnished. I ate in the comfortable dining room, and waited for Lesley's arrival by train and taxi.

Next day would see us firmly started on the Icknield Way stage of the walk. The Way is not one, but a whole complex of ancient tracks, used successively since neolithic times by Stone and Bronze Age peoples, by the Romans, and through the Middle Ages by drovers and tradespeople, down to their use today by modern travellers. A distinction needs here to be made between the presumed ancient track, marked with Gothic letters on the Ordnance Survey maps, and the Icknield Way Path, which is a walker's route devised by the Icknield Way Association. The path keeps to the general line of the old Icknield Way but avoids road walking as much as possible, by using other paths and tracks where the old Way has been obscured or taken over by roads. For now I would follow the path, which is waymarked for over a hundred miles to Ivinghoe Beacon, in Buckinghamshire, where it meets the Ridgeway National Trail and accompanies it into Berkshire and Wiltshire. I had the Icknield Way Association's Guide, but as it seems to be my fate to do long-distance walks the wrong way round, it was designed for the walker starting at the path's western end so yet again I was having to read a guide backwards!

The Icknield Way path takes a broad sweep south and east of Newmarket at a radius of about ten miles, and I soon discovered that I was probably the only person in Suffolk not to know that in this famous horse-rearing county there was a big race-meeting over the coming Mayday bank holiday weekend. My attempts to find somewhere to stay on Saturday were met with derision. 'You won't find anywhere to stay within fifty miles of Newmarket,' I was told. (I will draw a veil over other concurrent attractions such as the airshow at Duxford celebrating sixty years of the Spitfire in RAF service.) I was fast running out of ideas and having visions of being compelled to spend Saturday night huddled in some noisome outbuilding.

On the positive side I discovered I had walked a hundred miles, which seems a good point to end this chapter, with the future yet uncertain.

Barnham to Stetchworth

Chapter 4

Adventures of the joyful kind

On a cold blustery morning we set out to walk the long mile to Euston village (Yes, the same as the station.) At a busy crossroads we met our first waymark of the Icknield Way, a fingerpost bearing a reproduction of a Stone Age axe. A sandy track led into sweet-smelling pine woods and thence into open country, past a pig farm where a large pig waited in a trailer - was it to go to market, we wondered. Ahead two hares chased each other across a grassy field.

We came into woodland and looked for somewhere to stop for elevenses; two other walkers overtook us, on a day walk in our direction, and we lamented the dearth of convenient pubs. We were within earshot of the A134 road, and on learning of my intention to walk to Wales, one of the walkers said, 'But can you ever get away from traffic noise?' Lesley answered, 'Yes, but it's become more difficult.' I was often to remember their words as I tried to avoid the A40 trunk road.

Reaching the main road we put on waterproofs in the face of increasing wind and drizzle. An unavoidable mile along the A134 brought us to more long tracks through fields and woods, and, suddenly to where winter gave way to spring as we walked between grassy verges crammed with bluebells and cowslips towards a long avenue of scented purple lilacs. We lost count of the number of rabbits we saw. We had somehow missed a turning and this meant a roadwalk to West Stow, where we were directed by a lorry driver, who brought out his map to show us tonight's destination Hengrave, on a main road two miles south of where our map ended, and well off route. The quarter-inch map would have helped, but I'd left it at home thinking I'd have no further use for it.

We came after what seemed a long way to a junction where a signpost read ***Hengrave ¾ miles*** but an adjacent sign said **Road Closed**. Dismayed, we swithered around, wondering if we might come on some unfathomable chasm if we persisted down the road. Yet another lorry driver, seeing our confusion, asked if he could help. He was a small chubby man talking with a broad Suffolk accent. Oh yes, the road had been closed eighteen months or more, a rickety bridge, and the council wasn't going to repair it, but 'You go along there, my dears, nice and pretty.' It was, indeed, a delightful walk, past old houses at first, through woodland and over a dear little footbridge and the inevitable long search for Minstrels, next to the village hall and opposite Hengrave Hall, a Tudor mansion with an even older church.

We were dismayed to find that the nearest pub was a mile distant along a busy road, and our hosts were obviously in category one, expecting that we would think nothing of a two-mile walk after a day in the open, ignoring our hints that a lift might be appreciated. It wasn't a particularly peaceful walk, and The Greyhound was tucked away out of sight in the next village, but the friendly landlord offered and gave us a lift back to Minstrels after assuring us that he 'hadn't had a drink', an answer to an unspoken question I wouldn't have dared to ask.

We took a taxi back to West Stow next morning, still unsure where we would lay our heads that night. I'd lost count of the unsuccessful telephone calls I'd made. We walked along an avenue of trees and into fields through farmland. We passed Weatherhill Farm, which does offer accommodation, but not tonight, it was explained apologetically; there was a daughter's wedding. I'd become accustomed to being informed of family affairs disrupting provision of B&B: weddings, visits from long-lost relatives from far places, and sometimes, sadly, illness or bereavement.

We came past the church into the small village of Icklingham just as The Plough was opening and ordered double coffees and sandwiches. The saloon bar filled with well-dressed locals talking about the events of the weekend, notably the hunt which was coming through the village. Outside, in our quest for yet another telephone box, we saw pink coats disappearing down a lane. This time at Lesley's suggestion we tried Bury St Edmund's, a few miles off route to the east but with a train service which would take us there.

The proprietor of the guesthouse had only one single room vacant but was persuaded to let us also have the room belonging to her son who was away for the weekend. Relief!

The route led across the open heathland of Cavenham Nature Reserve where birdwatchers were 'looking for wheatears,' one of them said, and into Tuddenham, where it was now lunchtime, and the pub was full of jolly people celebrating a fine Saturday. Things took a turn for the worse. Once again we had a section without having recourse to a map. This seems like terminal carelessness, but the section was less than three miles and I'd thought that with the help of the guidebook we'd manage.

Perhaps it was the effect of too much tea at the pub, or just the after-lunch torpor which can affect one's judgement, but we came to a stile where we should have turned right along a track by a hedgerow but instead continued ahead along the more obvious track across a field. I discovered the mistake soon enough but instead of turning back at Lesley's suggestion (usually the best thing to do) I declared confidently that we could easily find our way back to the Icknield Way using the compass.

We came to a gate and a lane and turned right, then to another lane and turned left. We passed a raised reservoir, its waters deep blue with seabirds flying over, climbed a hill and emerged onto a vast prairie, a checkerboard of fields bordered by ditches and rather indeterminate earth tracks. Pieces of farm machinery lay around as if abandoned in a hurry. I was beginning to wonder if my optimism had been excessive.

Lesley suggested that we take a breather and assess our situation, which would of course have been sensible. But in this sort of crisis situation I suffer a build-up of adrenalin which makes me reluctant to stop for long, so after five minutes I headed in the direction where I was sure we would find the Icknield Way. We passed a small hut which seemed to have some connection with the Water Board and had a disconcertingly deep hole beside it, and headed for a wood. We turned a corner into a field and found that the track seemed to have vanished. If I had but known it (but was only to discover later) across the field and through a gate a few yards away on the other side of the wood ran the Icknield Way! But at this point my nerve failed. 'Perhaps we'd better turn back,' I said. So we did, retracing our steps for two or so miles and coming to the village of Herringswell where we should have been about two hours ago.

From leaving the pub at Tuddenham to arriving in Herringswell we had seen no person and no vehicle and the only dwellings had been a barn and the little waterworks hut. This gave the whole episode a dream-like quality as if some unspeakable calamity had claimed the lives of the population and we were the only survivors. The fact that we heard but didn't see the Duxford Spitfires passing over only enhanced the feeling of being alone in some uncharted wilderness.

We arrived at Bury St Edmunds in an advanced state of exhaustion and found the guesthouse. But despite a hurried turnaround for baths, we found that the pub had stopped serving meals, so we had to buy a picnic from the Jet petrol station and eat it in our room: crisps, pasties, cheese sticks, and yogurt and fruit, with Ovaltine to drink.

We caught the train to Kennett next day, Sunday. 'No one goes to Kennett,' said the guard who came to sell us tickets. 'The only thing worth seeing is the nineteenth-century signal box.' Certainly we found little else beside at the end of an eleven-minute journey. There was not even a railway bridge. We waited for the train to leave and crossed the line, confident that there were two hours to wait before the next train might be coming along. A keen wind was blowing - it seemed from Siberia. Having suffered intense mortification on finding how close to the Icknield Way we had been the previous day ('At least you were going in the right direction, said Lesley kindly) we'd decided to walk back and join up our route from the point where we'd left off. So we headed north, went past yet another pig farm, and came to a broad track which could only be the Icknield Way. Just two hundred yards along it we found a gate into a wood, and through it saw the shape of the little hut we had passed yesterday.

With honour satisfied we sat by the gate to have second breakfast, even seeing other walkers go by. We continued down the track into Kentford, where The Cock Inn was a rather unprepossessing road-house type of place too near the main road. The pub was full of Sunday drinkers, and it seemed that unescorted women of a certain age weren't welcome; Lesley had difficulty in getting served.

We diverted from the Icknield Way down a path by the Kennett river, and into Moulton near its packhorse bridge. Spring was advancing, there was ladysmock in the verges and the countryside was putting on its most vivid greens. Early, we sat on the village green watching a father and two children playing with the horse tethered there, until it got too cold and we walked by the side of the river through this picture-book village with its thatched cottages and bright gardens. St Peter's church on its hill looked interesting but was locked. We found another bridge and a family of ducks, and made yet more unsuccessful telephone calls, and finally arrived outside the gate of 6 The Street where Mr and Mrs Bolus were just returning from their round of golf and complaining about the weather. It had been too cold for comfort at Newmarket races yesterday they said.

We rejoined the Icknield way next morning in Chevely, where cyclists were starting a sponsored ride for multiple sclerosis, four hundred of them, someone said. Chevely was a friendly place, the shop was open and I was able to buy a replacement comb. The route started down a path between fences with gardens on one side and fences enclosing a stud farm on the other. An elderly man wearing a straw hat and wielding a hoe asked where I was going, and didn't seem to think much of the idea. He asked my age and on being told said with an air of triumph, 'I'm eighty-five.' It was hard not to conclude that there was an unspoken, 'I didn't get where I am today by walking to Wales.'

I went on wondering if I would still be pottering in my garden in ten years' time, always supposing that I should not have joined the great congregation of walkers in the sky. It is probably only the very young, like our three-year-old grandson Jamie and the very old, like our friend in his garden, who are able to take pride in counting the years. The rest of us do the best we can to fumble our way through that inexorable process of change which is called living while trying to hold on to an identity, the sense of having 'the same being', in the face of the numerous expectations and stereotypes held by others. Birthdays may mark the passsage of time, but make little difference to the way we feel about ourselves. I don't think that I felt pride on having attained three-quarters of a century earlier in the year, only a sense of wonder at the perfidy of time, which can lull one into the belief that it draws from a limitless store then comes like a marauder in the night to steal away the years one by one.

> Even such is time, which takes in trust
> Our youth, our joys, our all we have
> And pays us but with earth and dust.   Walter Raleigh

There must be loss involved in growing older, but I have always believed that there are consolations too, not least in being able to choose how to spend one's third and fourth ages freed of the responsibilities of the middle years.

> For age is opportunity no less
> Than youth itself though in another dress
> And as the evening twilight dies away
> The night is filled with stars invisible by day.
>   H.W.Longfellow

Leaving our friend tending his garden, we were soon back in arable farmland, rolling fields with oilseed rape now in bloom and, for once the sun shining. The route led through fields and woods and down into the cleft of the Devil's Ditch, one of the five long protective dykes which lie at right angles to the Icknield Way. The Devil's Ditch was once an important defence but is now just an easily surmounted overgrown cleft, two steps down and two steps up.

We came into Stetchworth and found the Marquis of Granby pub where the bar was full of young men drinking their way through the afternoon, but the barmaid found us some coffee and didn't charge for it.

Our lodging for the night was a suite of rooms in a lavishly appointed house full of antique furniture and paintings and bearing witness to Mrs Reed Herbert's love of horses. Like many 'horsey' people, our hostess seemed to be fonder of horses than of humans, treating the latter as necessary distractions in an otherwise perfect world - but our accommodation was comfortable and like most of our B&B's, blissfully quiet. The Marquis of Granby didn't serve meals, so we walked instead a three-quarter mile to the King's Head, no hardship on a balmy evening with white campion coming into bloom in the verges, and a peaceful friendly welcome when we arrived. After returning we watched *Ballykissangel*, a final and very moving episode.

We had early breakfast so that Mrs Reed Herbert could drive to her work in Newmarket (something to do with horses), taking Lesley with her to catch the London train. I left in the opposite direction for the next stage, which would take me out of East Anglia and into the Home Counties.

Stetchworth to Ickleford

Chapter 5

A Turning Point

I was now approaching a point of no return on my walk. In three days' time I would reach Royston, the first of a group of towns which confront the invading North London sprawl on the verges of a constantly threatened green belt. The Icknield Way path weaves a route through these towns while attempting to avoid as much of the built-up town centres and housing estates as possible; this is often commuter-land as well as having industrial bases of its own.

Some of the course of the true Way in these regions is used extensively by today's travellers, where macadam has replaced green turf, but they are merely using thoroughfares travelled over the centuries. Royston is sited at the junction of two busy main roads, the A14 to the north and the A10 to the south which follow the courses of the Icknield Way and the Roman highway Ermine Street. Each town has a tale to tell of past history. Hitchin is featured in the Domesday book as the manor of William the Conqueror; Dunstable was an important trade route and crossing place of the Icknield Way and Watling Street. Even in modern Letchworth Garden City remains have been unearthed of neolithic, Iron Age and Roman settlements. Luton, better known nowadays for its car factory and airport, has a museum housing many archaeological finds.

While negotiating this stretch across the Home Counties I would be less than fifty miles from home, and was planning to travel there for a two-day break. After this the distance from home would be steadily increasing.

On the Tuesday following the Mayday Bank Holiday I said farewell to Lesley in Stetchford, and then waited for the Community Centre to open at nine so that I could post a parcel home. This is a place where Post Office and small store survive only with the help of volunteers, with just one part-time worker employed to pay out pensions. The stile and waymark were just across the road, and led me along a green track. On the other side of a fence were racehorses and their foals, quite breathtakingly beautiful, standing or moving effortlessly in postures which made me think inevitably of ballet dancers. I began to have some inkling of what invokes a passion for racehorses in people.

The path did some intricate manoeuvres over stiles, through more fields - many containing head-high oilseed rape. I came to Burrough Green and took the Rider's route of the Icknield Way (no stiles) to Brinkley where I diverted to the King's Head for coffee.

Although I was the only customer, it was clear that the place was thriving, with its large dining room and extensive menu. The friendly landlord told me he had moved from Wembley eighteen months ago after years in the motor business. He called his wife and daughter into the bar to hear about my walk to Wales. 'How far do you walk in a day?' they asked, and, 'Aren't you afraid to walk by yourself?'

I walked down the road to pick up the path, and met a young woman leading a horse and saying something about being lame. I thought she meant me, but it was the horse having trouble with a rear foot.

Through more oilseed rape I went. This ubiquitous crop, beloved by farmers because well subsidised, was not so beloved by me as a walker, encroaching upon paths, obscuring the view, and making me sneeze. I went uphill, then along broad tracks between fields and looking westward saw a blue line of distant hills, forty or fifty miles away. With a lift of the heart I knew this was where I was going, and that there would be other hills beyond. It didn't matter that these were low hills - they were hills that had been seen over centuries by users of these ancient thoroughfares and I was thrilled to know that I was following in their footsteps.

The track did a squiggle to meet a road, and follow it into a little valley. Here I found a spot out of the wind to eat lunch before turning into the splendid green track Fox Lane, a long three miles leading into the outskirts of the Cambridgeshire village of Balsham. A cold rain set in and I needed more than one rest to get me into town as schools were turning out.

Balsham is a busy place which has managed to hold on to its shops and services, and is also ancient, having been first settled in Saxon times. The Icknield Way Association have erected a milestone on the village green which told me that I was sixty-three miles from the start of the Way at Ivinghoe Beacon. Except that the Beacon would for me be the *end* of another stage of the walk, and the *start* of the Ridgeway path.

I went through the churchyard and found my B&B near the garage, as I had been directed. My lodging for the night was a little self-contained flat next to the house, and for once I was offered an evening meal, now a rarity in the world of bed and breakfast. This once universal institution is in slow decline. Eating habits have changed considerably over the years, with greater choice of food in pubs and restaurants, and more people being accustomed to eating out. I rather suspect that the landlady offering full board is becoming an endangered species, and that many proprietors themselves no longer enjoy cooking for their guests. Mrs Greenaway had moved with the times in offering a choice of menu, with the help of another aid: the now universal deep freeze. I ate lasagne with a large salad with gooseberry crumble to follow, in generous helpings.

The garden, full of aquilegias, forget-me-nots, primroses, cowslips, lilacs and wallflowers, a mixture of the wild and the cultivated, looked as if it had been allowed to grow naturally but I guessed it was actually by design. Mrs Greenaway (what an appropriate name for a gardener!) confirmed that she had worked on making a wild cottage garden. She told me that she had an acre of land where she was creating a wildlife pond. Her thirteen-year-old son was a child actor, commuting daily to drama school in London and giving her plenty of work in providing transport to auditions and performances.

I managed to set up two more nights' B&B (the owner at Royston asked if I was attending the passing out parade!), and discovered that by the next day I would have completed fifty miles of the Icknield Way.

When I rose to make tea next morning, all the lights went out - which wasn't a good start to the day. The way out began in the centre of Balsham down Wood Hall, past cottages and along a short stretch of Roman Road. A green track led uphill to a water tower, thence down a steep rocky bridleway which deteriorated into deep mud.

In Linton I left the Icknield Way in an attempt to find a coffee shop, but the pretty main street boasted only closed restaurants, and a fish and chip shop in addition to the usual array of building societies and travel agencies. I crossed a busy main road and came to the gates of Linton Zoo where I was asked for an entrance fee of £3.75 to gain access to their cafeteria. Deciding that this was too much to pay for a cup of coffee, I walked on to the sign saying *Great Chesterford, Public Bridleway 4*. There would be no coffee break today but I had cold tea in my waterbottle and the remains of my full English breakfast brought from Balsham. It was a fine day and a long straight track led invitingly upward.

After a while the track entered a deep-cut furrow between fields, with thorn hedges, now in full bloom, on either side. I pushed my way through a tunnel of vegetation, luxuriantly growing swathes of cow parsley which caught at my fleece jacket and spilled petals on to clothing and boots. It felt claustrophobic, but I could sense that I was approaching a summit and after a while I emerged on a hilltop near a triangulation point and saw again that blue line of hills now becoming closer. There was a strong south-west wind blowing in my face as I descended the track to Burtonwood Farm, then through more oilseed rape. Traffic noise intensified, coming from the M11 motorway on the other side of the valley.

Great Chesterford's name testifies to its origin as a Roman fort of which no trace remains; the village boasts just a few thatched cottages, church, pubs and village hall, and, I was glad to see, a village store. I had received instructions which sounded complicated but in the event I found Mill House easily, by the river as the name suggests. The river is shown on the map as 'Cam or Granta', surprisingly. Did the mapmakers disagree about the name I wondered?

Mill House stood by itself in gardens, a Victorian House one hundred and fifty years old and, Mrs King told me, in the same family for a hundred years. I was shown to a splendid bedroom, perfectly designed for total relaxation: large and furnished with antiques, including a rocking-chair in front of a vast bay window overlooking a walled garden, clematis, lilacs, laburnham, lawns, a fishpond and a colony of rooks. In the distance I could see traffic on the motorway on the other side of the valley, but by some acoustic trick I heard no sound. I thought I could have stayed there all evening just watching the light fade, but after a while I roused myself and went to the shop. Alas, they had no bananas, but I bought yogurt and crisps and a frozen salmon dish which, being tired of pub meals, I asked Mrs King to prepare in her microwave for me.

There were two businessmen guests beside myself. Walkers don't seem to be very much in evidence although Mrs King said she had recently had a guest who was walking round the county of Norfolk using long distance footpaths. I rather wished I could have met an occasional wayfarer; being the only walker on a long-distance path sometimes felt a bit lonely. But Mrs King was so friendly and encouraging I felt warmed and strengthened and next morning became so engrossed in talking that I left later than I had intended. I had asked Mrs King if she didn't find the motorway disturbing at only a quarter-mile distance, but she spoke of the relief from dangerous through traffic which its arrival had brought to the village. I was made to realise that there are two sides in the debate about the building of new roads, and that the day-to-day quality of life of people may be equally as important as the long-term concerns of those who wish to preserve our countryside against devastation by new roads and concrete.

I left carrying a large parcel of sandwiches; Mrs King refused to charge for my packed lunch 'since I had had no breakfast'. I crossed the bridge over the river, then the one over the motorway; although I was still in Cambridgeshire this felt like a boundary, because tonight I would be in Hertfordshire. The way led steeply uphill through more engulfing cow parsley and once again debouched on a hilltop. I was enjoying these contrasts between being enclosed, hemmed in by ancient plantings, and finding myself on the cultivated prairies with their wide views and endless sky, and the blue line of hills coming ever nearer.

I had a long walk today so did some short cuts from the guidebook route, using country lanes rather than field footpaths to take me through a sequence of villages: Strethall, Elmdon, Chrishall and Heydon. There was the virtual absence of traffic I was becoming accustomed to on these country roads, but it seemed a long way, and I arrived in Heydon sore-footed and rather dismayed to find I was barely halfway to Royston. I sat on the village green and found that I was only a few miles away from Fowlmere, where my friends Sandra and John Betterton live. Thinking of arranging a meeting I found a phone box and left a message with the telephone number of that night's lodging.

The afternoon went better but it was a fifteen-mile day and I was relieved to come into Royston around rush-hour time. I tried to match the directions I had received with the confusion of the one-way traffic system, and as I stood by the roadside wondering which way to go a voice addressed me by name.

'I thought there wouldn't be two ladies carrying a rucksack,' said Mr Little, the proprietor of Greenways, which was just across the road, through a gate in a high garden wall. There was a message too, from Sandra, to say that they would come for me that evening. To meet with these two good friends relieved my tiredness immediately. John drove us to the village of Melbourne for a pub meal, and we talked about my walk and the countryside which they knew well. I was so touched to find how much they had been thinking of me ever since I had started walking. John then drove us to look at Therfield Heath where the Icknield Way path went but I had decided not to go tomorrow. It was a fine golden evening and the downs looked so lovely in their green mantle that I was tempted to change my mind, but I had other plans.

On the Royston by-pass I saw my first supermarket since leaving Cromer - a Tesco.

Between Royston and Baldock it is possible to avoid walking along urban streets by using the diversions the Icknield Way Association have cleverly devised to take their path south of the area. I chose instead to use public transport to take me to Letchworth where I would rejoin the route.

So next day, Friday, I took the train the short journey through Baldock to Letchworth, the original garden city, where I had never previously set foot. But the town centre looked little different from many others in England, with its multiple stores and High Street banks. I followed the railway line in a westerly direction to find a road sign directing me to Icknield Way, and thence to a suburban street lined with semi-detached houses: "Icknield Way" said the street sign. I came to a cemetery with seats under the trees and sat there to eat the last of Mrs King's sandwiches.

Across the road a footpath led across a field then another road, and to a hilltop, the site of Wilbury Iron Age hill fort. In the distance were the hills I had been approaching for almost fifty miles, green now with streaks of white betraying their chalk origin. The morning had been grey and misty, but I was now in hot sunshine. The path led downhill through fields with growing crops, across a railway (beware of fast trains) and into the little dell occupied by Gerry's Hole - a pond next to the railway embankment where - it is said - Gerry, one of the navvies who built the railway, had perished one dark night on his way home from the pub.

Over the gently flowing river Oughton I went and into Ickleford village opposite the handsome church. The timetable at the bus stop told me that there was a bus to Hitchin in ten minutes.

Many people haven't heard of Ickleford, which is a Hertfordshire village just a handful of miles from Hitchin, but it's a pretty place in itself, with some fine old buildings. It's a friendly place too. The woman who joined me at the bus stop asked how far I had walked and went on to tell me about a recent holiday at Ullapool in Sutherland, one of my favourite places. It was, therefore, in Ickleford that I realised that the walk in fact was going quite well, and that I had every chance of finishing it. Until then I had been unsure about how much I had wanted to go on. I seemed to have spent most of the time when I wasn't walking using the telephone in often despairing attempts to find somewhere to stay and this becomes wearying. For the first time ever on a long-distance walk I had sometimes felt lonely.

I discovered however that, despite a slow pace, I had walked one hundred and sixty-seven miles - about a third of the distance from Cromer to St David's Head in Pembrokeshire. Without doubt it would have been crazy to give up, and at this point I realised I didn't want to do so; it no longer became a question of 'if I reach St David's Head', but 'when'.

The notion of this being a turning point seeped into my consciousness only gradually as I took the bus to Hitchin and caught a train home, which took me just two hours. In the two days at home I planned ahead for the next stage to Gloucester, and did maintenance of myself and kit, changing winter walking gear for clothes more suitable for the summer which seemed to have arrived. My Brasher boots, now showing more signs of wear, I decided would do for at least the next stage.

I was dismayed to find I had been losing weight, ha thought I'd been eating well. I arranged a rendezvous with Sally who was to join me on the Ridgeway and tried to stifle my guilt about Dick being left to deal with the full burden of house and garden at a particularly busy time of year. I slept a lot too. Leaving home again was still a wrench but I realised that I was feeling fitter than when I started in April, and I was looking forward to the next stage. I still had some of the home county built-up areas to negotiate, but after these would come the Chilterns, the Berkshire Ridgeway, and the Cotswolds, with Wales waiting beyond. There was much to look forward to.

Ickleford to Monks Risborough.

Chapter 6

Going, Going...

Look, stranger, on this island now
W.H.Auden

Somewhere at King's Cross there was the unusual sound of an engine getting up steam and at the next platform was a string of assorted historic coaches. At every station along the way to Hitchin a crowd of people, mostly families with children, waited with camcorders at the ready and I learned that this was because the famous engine "Blue Peter" was coming this way. I could see faces fall when it turned out to be just an ordinary suburban train coming into the station!

I took a taxi from Hitchin station and talked with the driver about Norfolk, where he liked to fish, and realised that the memories of those parts of the walk were fast fading, overladen with what had happened since. I knew I would recover the memories when, some time in the future, I would be able to put the walk together as a complete whole rather than a succession of disconnected parts.

In warm sunshine I was back outside the George Inn in Ickleford by ten-thirty, where a group of ramblers was waiting to start a walk. I was quickly away from houses and into typical Icknield Way country: long straight tracks now becoming chalkier. I joined a busy main road for a few yards and met people on yet another charity walk - for Luton

Rotary Club today - mostly groups of cheerful youngsters dressed in bright summer wear.

The track climbed on to downland and around the slopes of Deacon Hill, where there was a dazzling view across miles of the Bedfordshire plain. I climbed again to cross one of the many Telegraph Hills to be met in high places. (The site of one of a chain of old telegraph stations stretching from Great Yarmouth to the Admiralty building in London.) There was a fine view from here too, and marshals for the charity walk were basking in the sunshine. Everything smelt good, the hawthorn, the oilseed rape and the mown grass, and the cuckoos were in full voice: 'In May I sing all the day'.

I came to a road and car park where people with picnic baskets were taking advantage of one of the first warm Sundays of the year. Another green lane brought me to the golf course on the outskirts of Luton. So far today's walk had been easy and enjoyable but I was soon to find myself in the midst of a new housing estate where the guidebook made no sense and I had a difficult time extricating myself. I found my way eventually to a recreation ground and crossed yet another Icknield Way town road to meet the white swan waymarks of the Lea Valley walk.

This was a local walk following the course of the Lea river from its origin and was a good idea for a way to take the path through Luton's suburbs. On this warm Sunday afternoon the expanses of green were busy with playing children, young families and people walking their dogs, but it was the sort of urban open space where the long-distance walker feels totally out of place. I tried to make myself invisible as I followed the path to meet an unbelievably congested and depressing traffic complex at Luton Leagrave station.

I'd walked fifteen miles and this I decided was enough for one day so I engaged the station taxi to take me to Dunstable, a mere three miles distant. I wasn't so sure that this was a good idea when I found myself in a scruffy privately-owned car with its upholstery dirty and falling apart and a driver who spent the whole journey talking on his mobile phone. My spirits sank further on arriving at Northway Guest House, which was on Watling Street, the main A5 road. I must have passed it many times on journeys to Wales. There was an unprepossessing front facade and litter in the short front garden. Inside, however, it was better; my room looked out on a secluded rear garden and there was an absence of traffic noise - although I had to run the gauntlet of lorry drivers clad only in towels in the unisex shower. There were food shops open just opposite and I was able to buy a picnic: pork pie, crisps and yogurt.

In town next morning three people separately asked me if I was lost! I was merely walking around looking at my map to find the place where the Icknield Way crosses Watling Street, because this seemed an important reference point. It appears, however, that carrying rucksack and stick and consulting a map throws out some kind of a signal identifying a person as different from the ordinary run of people going about their business and sure about where they are going. It makes one vulnerable to unsolicited offers of help. I began to feel self-conscious about looking at a map except when no-one was around, and began to rehearse suitable ripostes, for example, 'No, are you?'

Rejecting all offers of help, I managed single-handed to find the Icknield Way leading out of town. I climbed on to Dunstable Golf Course, where the view of the surrounding chalk downs unfolded, and the morning mist was clearing to blue skies and the promise of another warm day. On the Downs, owned by the National Trust, there was a Visitor Centre and the inevitable car park and people, but to compensate there was a snack bar where I had coffee and stayed a while to look at the view. The crowds dispersed as I followed a ridge steeply downhill looking towards where I thought Ivinghoe Beacon must be, and realising that I had reached the blue hills I had been walking towards since Balsham. I was coming to the end of another section of the walk.

A young couple watched me taking a picture and the boy asked, 'Will you take one of us?' - shushed by his female companion. I did of course, and wish I had their address to send them the print which shows them standing entwined against a brilliantly blue sky with the chalky hills as a backdrop,

I descended to follow a track around the perimeter of Dunstable Gliding Club, its machines grounded on this weekday, feeling relieved that I seemed to be shedding the London sprawl which had been so oppressive. I followed a bridle path and country lanes over a ford with swans and came into Edlesborough, where school was just turning out and I had a long search for a telephone. Ivinghoe Way, I found, was a half-mile outside the village, a new small housing development off a main road, and on the way to tomorrow's destination. The house is called Ridgeway End, another indicator of progress and the beginning of a fresh stage of the walk.

Although the Icknield Way path ends at Ivinghoe Beacon, the real Way, the one shown on the map in Gothic letters, continues its direction south-westward. In fact there are sometimes two Icknield Ways shown, an upper and a lower. Considerations such as weather conditions would have determined which route the old-time users would take. The long-distance walker, however, is directed on to the Ridgeway, which sometimes but not always takes the same line as the Icknield Way. (This is confusing, I know, but different people at different times have planned the long-distance trails and there has been a Ridgeway path for many years.)

To return to the Ridgeway: this is one of the oldest and probably most used National Trails. It ends at Ivinghoe Beacon after crossing the chalk downs west to east from Overton Hill near Avebury in Wiltshire through Berkshire to cross the Thames gap at Streatley, then the slopes of the Chilterns to Ivinghoe, passing many prehistoric sites on its way. (I realised that yet again I would be walking in an opposite direction to the guidebook route. I believe there is logic in this in that prevailing winds in Britain are deemed to blow west to east, but I can't believe that these ancient tracks weren't used by people walking in both directions.) I would have liked to follow the Ridgeway for its whole length, but at some point in Oxfordshire I would need to turn my steps north, while the Ridgeway would swoop to the south-west somewhere near White Horse Hill.

The Beacon next morning was invisible in thick mist which seemed reluctant to clear. So after taking a picture of my first Ridgeway fingerpost (black with white lettering and a familiar acorn emblem), I made haste to leave the ridge and escape into the plains of Buckinghamshire. This would be a forced march, as Wendover was rather outside my range, but once again it was where the accommodation was. The day was, on the whole, rather dreary, a process of taking short cuts along busy roads; at one point I found myself trying to overtake a series of huge circus trucks drawn up at a roadside and halting all the traffic, on what was described as the Icknield Way.

Every road sign I came to was pointing to Aylesbury. I came to a place called Bulbourne and, thinking that I might take a bus through Tring, I spent a number of my twenty pences talking to someone on the helpline who had never heard of the place! I decided that the walk was turning into a survey on public transport.

Finally, I found the Grand Union Canal, which had an arm going to Wendover and which had been provided with seats and information boards. With the sun now shining, the last two hours of the day were spent in restorative peace, with plenty of time to rest and look at the trees and flowers and ducklings. The canal path went through water meadows where yellow irises were coming into bloom and brought me out near the centre of town, where mindful that my B&B was said to be 'near the police station', I lost no time in seeking direction. It was a long walk, and I asked twice more, to make sure, but eventually 'even the weariest river winds somewhere safe to sea' I reminded myself. I turned into Lionel Avenue; the house was at the far end of course.

Mr and Mrs Macdonald were like a TV duo, taking turns in offering tea and comforting words; I felt too tired to go out to look for food, so had my last banana with the remains of my lunchtime corned beef roll bought from Edlesborough and fell asleep watching television. Next day, I decided, must be a rest day, or at least entail only a short walk.

Mr Macdonald drove me into Wendover next morning, a sad town centre in a pleasant small country town, where only a handful of shops remained open. But there was a Budgen convenience store where I could resupply myself with bananas. I joined the Ridgeway near the station, climbing into woods on the slopes of Bacombe Hill, but left it to descend into Butler's Cross. (By rights I should have gone through the grounds of Chequers, the Prime Minister's country house, but today was to be a rest day.)

I walked on to Little Kimble station, which was tiny, just a short platform on a single line. The next train would be at four pm (this was noon). I sat in sunshine listening to continuous traffic noise from the main Aylesbury road just behind the station and thought of the irony that a potentially environmentally friendly form of transport should be so under-used while polluting vehicles clogged main roads everywhere.

I took a footpath which shadowed the railway line, a bucolic scene, fields and hedgerows and browsing cattle, over stiles and a little river, and so to Monks Risborough station, where the platform was slightly larger and the next train was due in forty minutes. The station faced a modern housing estate where there was no sign of life, as if the population had fled some recent dire catastrophe. There was no guard on the train from whom I might have bought a ticket so the three-minute journey to Princes Risborough cost me nothing.

I walked in searing heat the few miles distance to Bledlow, musing on the apparently irreversible social changes brought about by our addiction to the motor car. My choice of route was inevitably taking me across a densely populated area of England where for many people a car was the only practicable means of getting about, to work, to school, for shopping and for personal contacts. I was continually seeing evidence of the changes wrought by the revolution in four-wheeled transport in less than fifty years, finding that communities were becoming virtually extinct, losing village store, post office, and pub, features around which the life of the community had revolved. There were new by-pass roads which seemed to have come out of nowhere, and with them had grown supermarkets and new housing developments.

I walked along a country road where fine new houses had been built. Each had its own double garage and wide lawns, where affluent families could enjoy having moved out of noisy town into peaceful country, and in doing so had destroyed the peace they were seeking, as well as taking away that peace from others.

As I walked through this new England I was grieving for what has been lost, while accepting that cars nowadays are as much a part of our daily life as are refrigerators and washing machines, and it would be equally difficult to imagine life without them. I think it is only in recent years that we are coming to realise there is a price to pay - and I imagine that the people who build tree-houses and dig tunnels in their attempts to prevent the building of new by-passes are giving the message 'We don't want to pay it'. Philip Larkin in 1971 foresaw what would happen when he wrote:

> It seems, just now
> To be happening so very fast:
> Despite all the land left free
> For the first time I feel somehow
> That it isn't going to last.

Thinking such sombre thoughts I walked into Bledlow, a large village with scattered housing and no appreciable centre. It boasts a manor house, a church and a pub - but no village store. I walked the three-quarters of a mile down West Lane as bid, and came to the spot where the lane met and crossed the lower Icknield Way, now a busy B road.

Cross Lanes Cottage was charming, a sixteenth-century house with gardens on three sides - pity about the traffic noise - but it was lovely inside and out. Mrs Coulter was on crutches after a knee replacement operation, but Mr Coulter brought me tea in the garden and offered an evening meal of shepherd's pie and bread-and-butter pudding prepared and delivered by members of the church's congregation in view of Mrs Coulter's temporary incapacity. I had to revise my views about the death of communities!

Rain and thunder woke me at seven - *rain before seven, fine by eleven,* I said to myself, but a temporary lull over breakfast (fresh grapefruit and poached egg) only lasted until

Mr Coulter had driven me back to the pub and I was launched on the Ridgeway path.

I was quickly into deep mud; parts of the Ridgeway are classified as RUPPs, *roads used as public paths*, or as By-Ways. Because such tracks are open to wheeled traffic, they are the source of conflict between walkers and drivers of four-wheel vehicles, and users of the path are asked on notice boards to respect the rights of other path users. Since all are legally permitted to use the path, there is little else that could be done. But heavy tyres have in places destroyed the ancient trackbed and I couldn't feel too respectful towards the perpetrators as I sloshed along.

Princes Risborough to Goring

The Ridgeway is wide at this point and contours around the wooded slopes of the Chilterns with occasional views of the Oxfordshire countryside below. I came to the tunnel which takes the Ridgeway under the M40 motorway, and stopped for a breather. I was now meeting other walkers and three of these came along as I was studying the map. 'Are you lost?' asked their leader, who was wearing a wide hat of the kind sported by Australians; all it needed was a fringe of corks to fend off the flies!

It was hard to imagine a place where one could be less lost, on a busy national trail going under one of the busiest motorways in the country, and I pointed this out. Just to make sure, however, I was shown on a strip map exactly where I was. I was more interested in where these walkers had slept the previous night, because I had no bed booked and was becoming worried about where I might find one. There was no room at Ewelme where I had hoped to go, and although there is a string of small towns along the Thames valley there seemed a dearth of accommodation in any of them. One walker I met tending his blisters had spent last night in a shack in Watlington. 'Nobody wants to do bed and breakfast any more,' he complained bitterly. 'People are too rich to need the money.'

Two young men I met further along were more helpful; they received my news that I was going to Wales with interest and gave me the number of Mr Smith of the Studio in Wallingford. He would, they said, come and pick me up from the path. I hadn't intended to go quite so far, but it seemed I would have to.

The rain stopped by lunchtime but it was so humid that even my Goretex waterproof refused to dry, and clouds were still low over the Chilterns - but I'd left the worst of the mud behind. I left the Ridgeway somewhere where it skated off in an easterly direction to join Grim's Ditch, an ancient fortification which once separated two kingdoms. I kept to the old Icknield Way, which eventually plunged me into horrendous rush-hour traffic near a busy airfield.

I came to a road junction at a place called Crowmarsh Gifford which seemed to have been designed with the express purpose of inciting motorists into mowing down pedestrians. But once I had escaped from the turmoil I found myself on the quiet outskirts of Wallingford, which had, amazingly, a surfeit of buses but little other motor traffic. I found a telephone box and called Mr Smith, who came within five minutes to pick me up, muddy boots and all.

Mr Smith eyed my battered boots with scorn, ignoring my account of their exploits in England and Scotland, not to mention that I had worn them since leaving Cromer. He, he retorted, still owned the boots he had worn in Germany when he had been with the British occupation force in 1948, the year of the Berlin airlift. These boots had been repaired I forget how many times but were still wearable. I obviously couldn't compete!

Mr Smith was a man of many parts. I worked out his age at seventy-one but found that he had the energy of a man twenty years younger, still running his picture-framing business 'minor royalty for customers' in addition to keeping the bed and breakfast business going. He was also something of a philosopher, telling me about his change of heart on the subject of war after seeing the devastation in Berlin. His latest project was learning to ride a mountain bike.

The fish and chip shop was too far, I said, so Mrs Smith cooked me chicken pie with chips and salad, devoured. I asked for eight-thirty breakfast - my usual time. 'But that's lunchtime,' protested Mr Smith, relenting on finding his other guest wanted breakfast at the same time.

By nine-thirty I was in Wallingford town centre, which had been pedestrianised. It was Friday, market day, and people were setting up stalls in the small square. I liked Wallingford, which had retained its small-town character and the shops I needed were all there, the post office to send maps home, a stationers to buy a map, and a small food store.

I had by now walked more than two hundred miles and was relieved to be leaving the Home Counties at last. In this part of southern England I couldn't escape the feeling that I was an intruder in an environment where people walked only because they couldn't afford to drive. If they insisted on walking they ought to be using those trails and paths designated for them and not cluttering up the roads intended for motorists. Were we becoming like America I wondered, where activities like walking were confined to National Parks?

Anyway, once past Goring-on-Thames, less than six miles distant, I should be in Berkshire, then Oxfordshire, then Gloucester.....

After yesterday's rain it was a cloudless morning promising to be hot and there was scarcely a ripple on the river Thames as I crossed the town bridge. The Ridgeway path, keeping faithfully to the ridge, had executed a rectangular excursion to the east before turning west down Grim's Ditch. I picked up the path after crossing the bridge over a new bypass not marked on my map, and met a group of young men wearing Fire Service logos. They were, they said, doing a thirty mile challenge. (I'd said, 'Don't tell me, you're doing a charity walk.') I should have remembered it was Friday and charity walks happen on a Sunday.

I found that I was now on the route of three waymarked paths: the Ridgeway, the Thames Walk, and the Swan Way. Where the Icknield Way went I had no idea. The Thames path is the most recently opened of the national trails, beginning at the Thames barrier in Greenwich and following the river to its source in the Cotswolds. I would meet the Thames path again later in the walk. The path made through fields, woods and a village, through a churchyard and on to the riverbank where it was too hot to sit in the sun. The river was busy with motor cruisers, a sculler with a cyclist and megaphone following, and people were drinking at the riverside pubs. Cows grazed in the fields, and the hedges were ablaze with hawthorn.

The path went through a private estate, where rabbits scuttled on immaculate lawns stretching down to the river, and deposited me in the centre of Goring, a small riverside resort. Gasping for liquid, I turned into a teashop, asked for lemonade and coffee, and ate carrot cake. I went to find my B&B, which was a half-mile outside town.

Leyland, which was the name of the house, was number three, Wallingford Road, but when I knocked at the door of number three, near the station, the nice person who came to answer it directed me further up the road. When I apologised for troubling her, she said, 'I don't mind, because the people who come here are so nice'!

I continued down the road as directed and after asking once more came through a rear gate to Leyland, where Mrs Wiltshire was busy dealing with builders who were working on outside scaffolding.

I bathed, and returned up the road towards the station to meet my friend Sally who was going to be my escort for the weekend. Sally, too, had been through the same search process as I had, calling in at number three and being offered a telephone to ask for directions. The journey from London on the hottest day of the year so far had been a sore trial for Sally, since the privatised Chiltern Railways had been badly delayed with a broken-down train, so Sally was heartily pleased to reach Leyland.

We made haste to walk into town to the Barleycorn Inn, which was busy but friendly and had a good and varied bar menu. We looked forward eagerly to the morrow when we would be on what I think of as being the best part of the Ridgeway, which goes along a high ridge in open country. The last time I had been there was with Dick over forty years ago, in 1955, the year of our marriage. How much would the Ridgeway have changed in those years, I wondered.

Chapter 7

Oxfordshire Summer

Forget the spreading of the hideous town
Think rather of the pack-horse on the down

William Morris

We shared the breakfast table with another Ridgeway walker and a couple from Capetown in South Africa, who told us how much safer, cleaner, and less violent was England. Nobody, they said, would dare to go walking alone in their country.

It was sheer self-indulgence, but I had ordered a taxi to take us across the river to Streatley to the spot where we would pick up the Ridgeway, thus avoiding two miles of walking along urban streets. This meant that by ten-thirty we were climbing past Warren Farm and into open country as the mists were dispersing to give us a foretaste of the heat that was to come. Coming from this direction, the first several miles of the Ridgeway are uphill, leading to an altitude of something under two hundred metres. Not high by any standard, but, because of its position above the Oxfordshire plains to the north and low-lying country descending through Hampshire and Wiltshire to the south coast, the Ridgeway gives the essence of ridge-walking, the feeling of being on a roof-top of the world.

After seeing how the Home Counties had become like one vast suburb, I was fearing irreversible changes in this precious landscape. Forty-three years is more than half a lifetime, but perhaps there are some things that can't change. True, the track must be wider than when I had trodden it with Dick; the Ridgeway is one of the most used trails, and is shared with horse-riders, cyclists and the occasional car (to Sally's disgust, but even car-owners do have a legal right to use parts of the Ridgeway.) The black and white fingerposts were new, as was the occasional water-point, each with its dedication to some past user of the path, but essentially, the Ridgeway was the same, even to those reminders of the twentieth century - the Didcot cooling towers and the Harwell Atomic Energy Research Establishment smudging the view to the north.

In 1955, when I was newly engaged to be married, I had known the Ridgeway only as another wholly enjoyable walk, a means of spending time with a loved companion. I had known nothing of the Ridgeway's rich history, nor of the many ancient treasures to be found along its length. Encountering it again however, I found the memories of those long-ago days still shining brightly and enhancing the present with renewed happiness.

Such recollections made for a perfect day of a kind which will remain unspoiled in memory long after the dull and difficult days have been forgotten, and with a good friend this was the best of all kinds of walking. To make it even more perfect, this was Sally's introduction to the Ridgeway, and her delight in it enhanced my own pleasure. So with talk and laughter we shared our enjoyment of everything around

OXFORDSHIRE

Woolstone
Letcombe Regis
Hill Fort
White Horse Hill
East Hendred
A34
Ridgeway
River Thames
Goring
Streatley
NEWBURY

Goring to Woolstone.

us: the hawthorn now in splendid bloom, the woodland in that fresh shade of green which signals the first full onset of summer. Best of all was the long track striding ahead, unbounded by hedge or wire, 'free as the blue paths in the snowy heavens', as Thomas described it. A flock of lapwings flew into our path frantically giving their characteristic *peewit* call in the attempt to warn us off their nests in the next field. When we sat down by the wayside for lunch they ceased their cries as if satisfied that we meant no harm. Poor parents, in a state of perpetual anxiety.

There was a new tunnel under the busy A34 trunk road, whose traffic noise we'd been hearing for too long, and which followed us for even longer. People from a local art group had painted a mural on the tunnel walls telling us about the wool trade that once thrived in the small settlements on the slopes of the Ridgeway, and whose names still betray their origin in the processes of spinning and weaving.

We came to a car park on Bury Down where people were picnicking in their cars with the doors open to moderate the heat, and looked for the descending track that would take us to East Hendred - that night's destination.

It was rough going, steep and overgrown and too hot for comfort. We went by the perimeter fence of the Rutherford laboratory and turned on to a grassy path between lines of trees. Some little way along was a cage, baited with raw meat, and a magpie desperately fluttering inside. It was the work of a moment to lift the cage and release it. A few paces further I nearly stepped on a nest containing fluffy brown chicks, which scattered under our feet, and scolded myself for being a clumsy human.

It wasn't far then to Ridgeway Lodge, on a minor road coming down from the ridge and a half-mile outside East Hendred. This was a modern building in the throes of building work; a swimming pool was under construction. Our room had a breathtaking view out to the slopes of the Ridgeway, the afternoon haze clearing to show every crease and fold of the hillside in the late sunshine. We drank quarts of tea, bathed, and watched a memorial programme about singer Frank Sinatra, whose death had been announced two days ago - one of the few pieces of news which had got through to me. Later our host, Peter, drove us down to the village, the promised evening meal not having materialised, something about the cook being off duty.

The Wheatsheaf was a nice pub, patronised by Harwell workers and quiet even on this Saturday evening. The village of East Hendred was interesting too, with thatched houses, an old well and a sixteenth-century church. Peter said that the village was mentioned in the Domesday Book, and being away from the main road had escaped the attentions of too many visitors.

The only other residents at Ridgeway Lodge were people working or studying at Harwell, and this may explain the feeling we had of being rather out of place there in the absence of other walkers. This was surprising since the house was ideally situated and well equipped but Peter didn't seem to think that the Lodge had much part to play in catering for overnight Ridgeway walkers. Our feeling was that given adequate publicity there would be ample reason for walkers to use the Lodge, and we concluded that the regular custom of Harwell workers might be preferred - no muddy boots, for example.

It was a steep climb back to the ridge, where the car park at the road end was busy with Sunday visitors. We climbed on to Scutchamer Knob, a Saxon long barrow marking the county boundary between Oxfordshire and Berkshire. In the clear morning air we looked south over fields of growing crops across miles of English countryside to where Newbury was a smudge on the horizon. Further on we met two walkers doing a long training stage in preparation for a walk round the South West Peninsula Coast path, at five hundred and fifteen miles the longest National Trail in Britain. They'd read of me they said, in *The Rambler* magazine.

The track steadily rose and fell; we passed a traveller encampment with real horse-drawn caravans, and climbed towards a distant prominent spike which when we reached it was revealed as dedicated to soldier and Victoria Cross holder Robert Loyd-Lindsay Baron of Wantage and erected by his wife.

We were at last losing sight of the Didcot towers. It became even hotter than yesterday. Feeling hungry and thirsty we came to Segsbury Down and turned downhill to its hill fort. The proximity of a car park ensured that the large field managed by the National Trust and the hill fort occupying a prominent position on the edge of the escarpment had its complement of picnic parties, but this could not detract from the dramatic impact of the view to the north over what seemed like half of England. Below us was the best of English landscape, fields and hedgerows and woods, and somewhere in the blue the course of the Thames river, where I would be going after tomorrow.

As we descended the steep hillside into Letcombe Regis we began to meet participants in the fourth sponsored walk I had met in my five weeks on the trail. This one was in support of the village school, and had distances appropriate for all comers, families with young children as well as more experienced walkers. On this very hot day there was a fine selection of hats on show, from old-time straw boaters to more fashionable confections. We knew that our B&B hosts were doing the walk so went into the White Hart for coffee, found we were fortunate to get this as the pub was in process of being closed down; a divorce, we learned. Oh dear, I do seem to meet people suffering the troubles of life!

The Old Vicarage was just across the road, and we sat in the fine country garden in the shade of a mulberry tree to await the arrival of the walkers. The imposing house, with its ornamental brickwork, was built in 1840, and was on its fourth owner since the presiding vicar had moved to other accommodation. This round of owners was a young family with a father commuting daily to his health club business in Chiswick, but keeping going a thriving provision of bed and breakfast. No meal at the pub, alas, but we gratefully accepted an offer of soup and sandwiches, rather than trying to get into Wantage, the nearest place where food was available.

Early to bed, I awoke to find Sally standing by the open window, trying to expel a large and rather nasty-looking insect - a hornet we thought - which had been buzzing around rather alarmingly. With combined operations we managed to expel the intruder and subsequently slept more peacefully.

Next morning brought a farewell to Sally, who resolutely refused the offer from the Netherlands couple sharing our breakfast table of a lift into neighbouring Wantage on her way home. She preferred to extend the pleasures of her weekend by walking into Wantage for a browse round the town before taking the bus to Oxford. I set off in the opposite direction, past the church and to follow a muddy bridleway on a still cloudless morning.

Today, sadly, I was to leave the Ridgeway, which would soon turn in a south-westerly direction to head for the high country of the Marlborough Downs and Overton Hill where it approaches the celebrated stone circle at Avebury. I would continue only to White Horse Hill, another dramatic landmark on the route whence I would turn north for Oxfordshire and the Cotswolds. I had a rendezvous with Dick arranged for the end of the day.

In two hours I was back on the Ridgeway path and climbing again round the hollow of the Devil's Punchbowl. White Horse Hill above Uffington hides itself from view until the last minute, when the hill is revealed at the summit of a steep ascent. Less than a hundred feet above the ridge, White Horse Hill still appears as a real conical summit giving access to a three hundred and sixty degree view, of the track itself winding invitingly on in two directions, and the lesser fields and slopes below. The horse itself is invisible from the ridge; you have to be a traveller in the train hurtling towards Swindon or a passenger in a car on the road below to see the flying shape in full detail. The chalk-cut animal does not altogether meet the conventional description of 'horse'. Its elongated limbs suggest those of some prehistoric creature, as indeed it might be; nobody is quite sure of the age of the Uffington white horse, who it was who carved it out of the chalk, and to what purpose. For much of the following day we were to look back southwards and still see this mystical ancient artifact.

I joined lunchtime picnickers from the car park on the northern slope of White Horse Hill and spent a drowsy hour in the still hot sunshine, reluctant to leave this magical section of the walk. I had felt richly comforted by walking here where others had trodden for over four thousand years and in gaining the assurance that solitude and beauty could still be found in the over-crowded south of England. Sally had vowed to return to finish her Ridgeway and I was feeling that I too must complete mine some time in the future.

I came to the White Horse Inn at Woolstone, another old coaching inn, although no longer on a main highway; even the B road joining Wantage with Ashbury by-passes the village. I booked into my room in the converted stable block across the inn courtyard and went out to telephone for tomorrow's B&B. Dick met me as I returned, having travelled by train from London to Swindon, bus to Longcot, and field footpath to Woolstone. Another stage of the walk was about to start.

Chapter 8

Real Walkers

Between the south of England and South Wales there is a major obstacle in the shape of the River Severn, which rises in the mountains of central Wales on the mountain Pumlumon and flows along the England-Wales border and into the Bristol Channel. The two Severn toll bridges take the M4 motorway between England and Wales but north of the M4 the next crossing is at Gloucester where our soon-to-be encountered friend the A40 heads for Wales. Before the Industrial Revolution the river was thought too difficult and dangerous to bridge, and crossing south of Tewkesbury was by ferry only. The map shows many small roads crossing the river plain and coming to a sudden stop by places where there used to be a jetty and ferry. Even today people driving to Wales on the M4 may be obliged to make lengthy detours if, as occasionally happens, the Severn bridges are closed by adverse weather conditions.

Travellers of old would have crossed the Bristol Channel or Severn by coracle or boat in the absence of bridges, but for me there seemed to be no alternative to aiming for Gloucester via Lechlade and Cirencester, with a brief encounter with the Thames path en route, following in Roman footsteps in part. Once at Gloucester I would have to join west-bound traffic on the A40, but I hoped this encounter would be

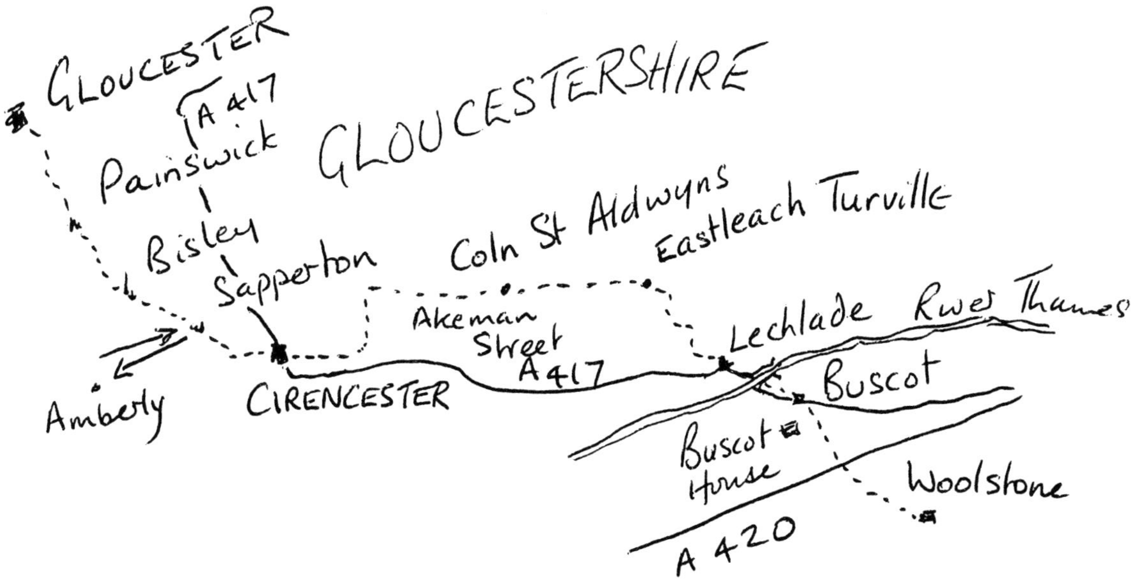
GLOUCESTER
A 417
Painswick
GLOUCESTERSHIRE
Bisley
Sapperton
Coln St Aldwyns
Eastleach Turville
Akeman Street
A 417
Lechlade
River Thames
Amberly
CIRENCESTER
Buscot
Buscot House
Woolstone
A 420

Woolstone to Gloucester.

short-lived. After the Severn bridge there was a path along the river going in the right direction.

It was still hot and sunny when we left the White Horse. For the first two miles we followed in reverse Dick's steps of the previous day, across fields where there was little trace of the footpath indicated by a fingerpost where it left the road. We were to find that in these parts the presence of a dotted line on the map did not necessarily guarantee a useable footpath. A right of way has to be walked and maintained to ensure it remains a viable means of getting about, and once fallen into disuse dedicated work is needed to rehabilitate a footpath. Although it is the legal responsibility of local authorities to maintain rights of way, the work is in practice left largely to groups of volunteers to look after paths, with the Ramblers' Association taking a leading role.

We went on by quiet bridleways, field footpaths and farm tracks, crossing just one main road on our way. This was perfect English countryside, in full late spring attire, the waysides bursting with vetch, cowslips and poppies, and much, much cow parsley. There were cultivated fields and rolling wooded hills and buttercups were coming into bloom in the pastures. We heard the cuckoo, which doesn't seem to live on the Ridgeway. On the western horizon we saw another thin blue line of hills which could only be the ridge of the Cotswolds.

There was a dearth of comfortable places to stop to eat, not a sign of a convenient pub, so we were relieved to find at the end of a long lane the grounds of the Buscot Park Cricket Club. No match in progress, but a welcome seat, shaded from the afternoon's heat by an oak tree. Buscot House and park are owned by the National Trust, but we were disappointed in our plan to walk through the grounds, finding the gates securely fastened. The eighteenth-century house, we discovered, is open to the public only at summer weekends. We had to take the alternative of a gruesome mile along the busy A417.

Buscot, the first Cotswold village we were to come to, was tucked away down a side turning, having honey-coloured stone houses, an old well, and, we were delighted to find, a shop selling groceries and picture postcards, and serving tea. So we had a large pot in the garden, before moving on round the corner to Apple Tree House, which was a very well organised B&B. We had hot baths and later took our evening drams into the garden, where Mrs Reay was busy weeding and complaining about the abundant growth of vegetation after the extra-wet spring.

We had a self-catering supper after learning that it was a mile walk to the pub, then for our evening exercise walked down in the gloaming to look at the river Thames. The lane led to Buscot Lock where there were a bridge, swans, weeping willows and a line of poplars, all reflected in mirror-still water. We were pleased to see that the National Trust, which owns the lock and surroundings, has closed the lane to cars.

Next morning we retraced our steps to the river where we crossed the lock and found the Thames path, which seemed to be going round in circles to get to Lechlade, so we left it as soon as we could. An essential footbridge is lacking near here, so Thames path walkers have to divert to a road bridge. We climbed a hillside, found stiles and a gate, and crossed a minor road to meet and follow a tributary, the river Leach. We were now walking in Tombs country, including the places where Dick's great-great-grandfather Edward had been born and met his bride Lucy and which at the recorded age of nineteen he had left in 1798 to enlist at Sherborne for a soldier career in the 11th Light Dragoons.

Edward Tombs served with his regiment for sixteen years, having an adventurous time, including a spell as a prisoner of war in Holland. He served in Spain in the Peninsular War, and was awarded a silver medal with bar for his service in the battle of Salamanca in 1812. Army records suggest that he was invalided out in 1814, receiving a permanent army pension until his death in 1848 at the age of sixty-nine. He did however, return to the Service in the 1820s.

A number of villages in the quiet countryside have been associated with my husband's ancestor. Kempsford, where his supposed parents - Martha and Thomas - registered his birth; Lechlade, to which his army discharge papers were made out; Quenington or 'Quinington', said in family papers to have been his birthplace; Alvescot, just over the border in Oxfordshire, where Edward lived with his first wife Lucy Longford and their son John, and later with his second wife Elizabeth; and Eastleach Turville, Lucy's birthplace, where we would go that day.

We followed a footpath along the river, through fields where horses grazed and over rickety stiles; finally we came to a field knee-high in growing wheat and without any perceptible way through, and forsook it for a country lane, one of an intricate network in an area without any major highways. We cooled off under the shade of umbrellas outside the Swan at Southrop, and later arrived in Eastleach Turville.

We turned down the village street, past what looked like a row of almshouses, climbed a hill, and found at its summit a war memorial with a seat under a tree close by. Here we sat to eat lunch and to talk about the past. In this quiet place and despite the evidence of later wars, it was easy to believe that little had changed since Lucy had lived here and met her soldier husband. The narrow road swooped downhill and turned a corner to cross a valley beyond green water-meadows, to rise again to a more distant hill. There was no sign of any other dwelling, just a board pointing to the parish church, where Lucy was baptised in May 1784.

There is a mystery around Lucy's birth. George and Mary Longford, shown in the baptismal register as her parents, had been married forty-three years before her birth, thus it seems more likely that they were her grandparents - so may have raised Lucy in the absence of her mother. The possibility is that Lucy's mother died in childbirth as did so many women of her century and furthermore, since no father was mentioned, the baby may have been illegitimate. Lucy, alas, had a short life, dying in December 1820, when her son John, was two years old and Edward was away on a second period of army service, having been recalled to the colours in 1819. Edward remarried in 1823, possibly in part to provide a carer for his motherless son.

John, by virtue of his father's army service and incapacity for work, was educated at what was to become the Duke of York's Royal Military School in Chelsea. At a time when it was rare for any working-class child, especially if living outside the big cities, to receive any but the most basic education, this was a privilege denied to many. Edward himself was illiterate. John left school at the age of fourteen to be apprenticed to a tailor, and later became the first of five generations of Tombses to work and live in London.

John seems at some time to have lost contact with his family, who continued to live at Alvescot for a while. John moved first to Bampton in Oxfordshire and later to London, where he lived in Gough Street, Saint Pancras, and founded a dynasty of London Tombses, siring seven children, one of whom, Henry John, was Dick's grandfather. The history of this one small family thus becomes in microcosm a social history of a whole Victorian middle class.

Knowing just a little about any such family history incites a great desire to know more, or to attempt to conjure up these people from the past and to talk with them. I thought, then, of Edward riding his horse along these country lanes and meeting his Lucy, perhaps where she worked on her grandparents' farm, conscious of her problematic status in a small community. I thought of the small family thrown into confusion by Lucy's death, and the small child wanting his mother; of the same boy at the age of nine sent away to school in the big city. With its mixture of disruption by war, family secrets, tragedy through death and advancement through migration from country to city, this tale seemed to be one that might have come from the pen of a Dickens or a Hardy. There was an especial poignancy in our reminiscences today, since earlier in the year we had attended the funeral of another Lucy, Dick's cousin and

Edward and Lucy's great-grand-daughter, who at eighty-nine had been the sole survivor of her generation.

We continued our walk along those same country lanes, climbing steeply to the village of Hathrop and later to Coln St Alwyn's. We asked a passer-by for directions to Deer Park Cottage where we were to stay, and were told, 'No more hills to climb.' He little knew, said I to myself, thinking of the hills of Wales.

Deer Park Cottage is on the boundary of a large estate in the village of Coln St Alwyn's. Our accommodation was in a small self-contained bungalow round the corner from the main house. Some noisy dogs in cages greeted us but quickly subsided at a word. They were being trained as gundogs, explained our hostess. We begged a lift into the village to shop, and later sat outside watching clouds gather in advance of a forecast change in the weather.

We shared the breakfast table with a young Japanese visitor touring the Cotswolds on a bicycle. Our hostess Mrs Bayliss came to talk about horses - they had two, and a foal. Mrs Bayliss interest is endurance riding, the horseback equivalent of long-distance walking, challenge events on bridleways over distances between five and a hundred miles. Mrs Bayliss was about to attempt her first twenty-mile event. On these events the horses have to be pronounced fit by a veterinary surgeon before competing, unlike long-distance walkers I thought, who have to look after themselves!

We walked into the immaculate village (even the telephone cabin was built of Cotswold stone) and crossed the Coln River to climb the hill into Quenington, where we took a bridleway through fields full of sheep and emerged on to a

Roman road. Akeman Street is a long road, traceable on the map to the east of Aylesbury in Buckinghamshire and reaching towards St Albans where it may have joined Watling Street. Westwards Akeman Street aims for Cirencester where it forms a junction with other Roman roads, notably the Fosse Way. The Gloucestershire Akeman Street is now a tarmaced country lane, so we had to share it with the light local traffic, using it as an alternative to the busy A417 to the south.

In true Roman fashion, the road kept to the high ground and on the whole away from dwellings. The grass verges, we noted, were being used for an experiment in wayside management; one side of the road was to be left uncut, said warning signs. At this point it was impossible to distinguish the cut from the uncut verges.

After some miles of this we left Akeman Street and descended into Ampney Regis, where the pub marked on the map was no longer in being but some passers-by directed us to the Crown Regis on the main road. This was a busy roadhouse crowded with lunching business people and coach-borne travellers. It didn't seem like our kind of place, but there was an outside garden, so we joined the queue at the bar and took our drinks outside to a table where we lunched overlooking the Ampney Brook, a charming stream with the usual complement of ducks. This brief contact with the motorised world over, we dodged the A417 traffic and found more country lanes.

The map showed a turning which should lead us to the outskirts of Cirencester, but reaching it we were alarmed to find a traffic sign saying *No through road.* The reason became clear after we had walked for a half-mile: the road was obstructed by a fence, but a new stile had been built; once over it we found ourselves on an embankment with steps leading down to a new dual carriageway road. We could see more steps and another stile beyond. This, we learned later, was a new link road between motorways M4 and M5 and providing relief from congestion in Cirencester. All we had to do was to escape being mown down by the heavy vehicles whose drivers no doubt had no expectation of needing to look out for pedestrians.

The approach to Cirencester was intricate, down a littered path by a culverted river, across another road complex, and under a grubby subway. But Victoria Street was just around the corner, a town street with about twenty bed and breakfast signs. We had a pleasant room at the back of the house overlooking a stonemason's yard. Recovered from the day's stint, we went into town, just five minutes' walk away and ate at the fish restaurant in the main street. We looked briefly at the fine parish church and wool market, and went sleepily to bed.

We were away early next morning for Dick to catch the Stagecoach bus to Swindon en route for home. I had some time to look around the town, which has a colourful Market Place with its buildings painted in blues, pinks and greens. The parish church of St John the Baptist is said to be one of the Cotswolds' finest 'wool churches', built during the great wool boom of the fourteenth and fifteenth centuries. The fan-vaulted south porch, overlooking the market square, gives the church a distinction such as a cathedral might possess.

Cirencester was once the second largest city in Roman Britain, although nowadays the only visible remains are its enclosing earth ramparts and an amphitheatre and quarry. My route out led along the stone wall which had been built to succeed the earth ramparts, and I turned a corner into the entrance to Cirencester Park. Unlike its built-up character on the east, the west side of Cirencester town has escaped development by the existence of this park, once a manorial estate, and still in the keeping of the Earl of Bathurst whose ancestors built the Manor House in 1714. The park is open to *pedestrians and horses only,* I read on numerous wayside notices - cyclists and motorists excluded.

From the park's imposing gates a wide avenue flanked by lawns and large shade trees, cedars, horse chestnuts, oaks led ruler-straight as far as the eye could see, parallel lines appearing to join somewhere in the distance. The few people out for morning exercise or walking their dogs soon fell behind and after a while the made-up path ended, to be replaced by an ill-defined grassy strand, lumpy and uneven underfoot as a result of its use by horses.

For six miles I followed these parallel lines in solitary enjoyment, looking for the landmarks shown on my map: the seat, dedicated to Alexander Pope, who with the first Earl Bathurst planned the landscaping of the park, and Ivy Lodge, where a polo club is based. Some spectators were gathered here and on a patch of lawn a rider in a pink jacket was exercising a horse and showing its paces, prancing and turning. For a quarter-mile the path joined an access road to the house, descending into a deep valley rather like a

Devonshire combe and climbing steeply to rejoin the parallel lines, mounting again as the track had throughout.

I came at last to what seemed like the summit: 176 metres, ten rides, said the map; yes, I counted ten grassy lanes disappearing into the trees. There was more to come; the way led over unfenced farmland, into the trees again, and ended against high iron gates, with a firmly closed lodge building behind them looking derelict. There was a way round, through some trees, over a trickle of a stream, and back into the same wide expanse of green, now overgrown, with only a narrow track leading the way, but this, by way of compensation, was a wild-flower sanctuary. After a while I came to a minor road, where there was a wooden barrier and another of those notices banning cyclists, and reminding me that I was using the path courtesy of the Earl of Bathurst.

It was just a half-mile into the village of Sapperton, where I was to meet Geoff, my host for the weekend. Geoff was an old friend from climbing days and I was responding to the pressing invitation from him and his wife Gill that I should plan my route to make it possible for me to visit them overnight. Sapperton was within easy reach of Gloucester and the Severn crossing, where I would break off the walk to travel home by train, for a mid-walk break. I was now committed to going on to Wales and looked forward to the prospect with pleasure.

I found a telephone box and interrupted Geoff and Gill at lunch, then repaired to 'The Bell' to drink coffee in the garden and to await Geoff who had a ten-mile drive from his house in Amberley, which I was to see for the first time. I relaxed in the comfort of Geoff's car as we drove through the lovely Cotswold country and climbed on to Minchinhampton Common past a golf course and over grassland where cows were feeding; the old custom of commoners' rights to graze their animals still pertains here, Geoff said.

Gill was waiting at the gate of Highstones, a splendid house built in the early twentieth century on a terrace overlooking the common and with a view over a valley west to the ridge of the Cotswold hills. This, I learned, is a butterfly house, so called because its construction resembles a butterfly's body, with a narrow central section and forward facing wings; most of the windows face the front view, with the rear of the house against the sheltering hillside. A wonderful sanctuary for a jaded walker, and my two nights there provided one of the highlights of the walk, being cosseted and well-fed, and with the opportunity for catching up with old friends.

Geoff and Gill are both keen walkers, and Geoff, who is good with maps, devised a route to take me to Painswick next day, Saturday, when Gill would walk with me. Geoff was to provide the transport in between gardening and doing the shopping. So back we went to Sapperton to pick up my route at the telephone box. I wasn't at all confident of finding the way; I was used to working with 1 in 50,000 Ordnance Survey maps of the scale one mile to one-and-a-quarter inches, whereas Geoff had used the 1 in 25,000, at double the scale, which I found difficult to follow, so we totally failed to find the first footpath on the route. It wasn't serious, since our way led us up a shady lane which seemed to have been abandoned by traffic. We found a footpath in the end, over stiles and through fields full of buttercups where no one seemed to have trodden since the winter. We came, eventually, to Bisley, which I had not heard of, but which turned out to be quite famous, an unspoilt Cotswold village with the second Seven Springs I had met in the area. (The first at Coberley near Cheltenham marks the source of the River Churn, one of the claimants to being the true source of the River Thames.)

There seems to be a lot about maps in this account of my walk, perhaps because much of it doesn't follow established long-distance routes which are usually well way-marked, so I was constantly choosing my own route, which needed frequent reference to maps.

Gill insisted I see the Seven Springs, but first it was coffee time, and, providentially, as we walked by the village hall in the main street, Gill was greeted by Katherine, who turned out to be her local parish priest. This was the church's coffee morning, with coffee and home-made goodies being served inside, and friendly people, who heard with interest about my walk. As we went on to talk about my earlier walk, I learned that there is a club for cyclists known as the Cape Wrath Club, where qualification for membership is having taken a cycle over the rough country to reach that far outpost of Scotland. I had done my share of cross-country cycling in the past, but think I would have drawn the line at Cape Wrath!

Seven Springs was just around the corner, ducks floating in the stone troughs, with spouts placed to catch water running off the hillside. The ceremony of well-dressing had been held on Ascension Day, two days earlier, and wreaths and bunches of flowers garlanded the rocky hillside. We walked through the churchyard and inspected the village lock-up, then left to find our way to Painswick. This was an interesting route, crossing the grain of the land, through woods and along a path winding round the hillside. At one point we lost the rudimentary path and found ourselves in someone's well-cared-for back garden.

To our apologies the owner replied, 'You're not the first', a reason I might have thought for some waymarking. This was complicated country, surprising me by the path's sudden changes of direction and succession of ascents and descents, with the countryside at its best, the trees their freshest green and meadows full of flowers. We finally climbed a steep hill and emerged on the road at Bull's Cross; cross in this context is a crossing point of routes, rather than a religious emblem. From here it was a half-mile into Painswick.

I had been here before on my walk north to south through England and Scotland, so this point where the two routes crossed was an important staging post for me. We stopped outside the church with its ninety-nine yew trees, and I suggested we name this place Joyce's Cross. We decided it was an occasion for celebration, so we went into Bertram's cafe for cream teas, while we waited for our transport. One of the customers, seeing our Leki sticks, said admiringly, 'You must be *real* walkers!'. As we left Painswick a light rain began to fall, the first I had seen since near Thetford - only a month ago, but it seemed longer. This was the beginning of the unsettled weather which I was to encounter for the rest of the walk.

Back in Painswick next morning I picked up the white circle waymarks of the Cotswold Way, taking me over the golf course and under the slopes of Painswick Beacon. I left the Way to descend through Upton St Leonard's then endured a dreary three miles through Gloucester's outskirts, so I was heartily glad to reach the station. The train took me through the country where I had already walked and past my old friend the White Horse, so I was able to reflect on the distance covered so far - almost three hundred miles, leaving me with less than two hundred to go to St David's Head. I couldn't wait to start!

Chapter 9

All the way to Wales

The soft feet of the blessed go
In the soft Western vales
The road the silent saints accord
The road from heaven to Hereford
Where the apple wood of Hereford
Goes all the way to Wales

G. K. Chesterton

My relationship with Wales has always been an ambiguous one; I've never been quite sure whether it is of love or hate. Wales is a wonderful country, with scenery unsurpassed anywhere in the world - from the austere and savage mountains of Snowdonia through the wild but gentler deserted mid-Wales counties to the scenic western coastline and the industrialised valleys of the south, with their history of hardship. Its people are of a race apart, with a language that sounds almost unearthly, sung rather than spoken. This capacity for song seems inborn in anyone of Welsh descent - even those who left the land of their fathers many years ago. Because so much of Wales is sparsely populated, the impression of its long past, dating back to pre-Roman times, is even stronger than in over-populated England, where so much ancient history has been overlaid with the constructions of a twentieth-century society.

I first visited Snowdonia as a child with my parents in pre-war days and remember being awed by its atmospheric beauty at the same time as being intimidated by its apparent inaccessibility to ordinary mortals. In post-war years I learned to climb on the cliffs of Snowdonia, and the area later became a place for our own family holidays in a small cottage once built and occupied by slate quarrymen. Tan-y-Graig is part of family history, and helped to develop in our children an enduring love for wild places.

With all this often intimate knowledge I still approach Wales with a feeling that I somehow have to watch my step, that there is an unforgiving element about this lovely country, which will keep its welcome in the valleys but will still hold itself aloof from complete acceptance of strangers. There is thus a challenge in entering and learning more of Wales, rather as one might feel about meeting a lovely but uncommunicative stranger whom one would like to know better.

And there is the weather, of course. At Tan-y-Graig there can be no more perfect place to be on a sunny afternoon than on its terrace facing the slopes of Snowdon. Along with such days you have to be prepared for others when the hills withdraw into their veils of cloud and the rain goes on for days. "If you can see Snowdon across the lake it's going to rain, and if you can't see it it's raining" goes the saying. It is, they say, the climate which gives Welsh people their lovely singing voices, and the landscape its fresh green, and I had grown over the years to accept wet Welsh weather as part of the whole experience of being there.

Wales has responded to social change in different ways across the country. For one thing, in the south it is rare to hear Welsh used in ordinary speech, whereas in Llanberis in Gwynedd it is commonplace to hear Welsh spoken in shops in ordinary commercial transactions. South Wales is a major industrial centre even though the collieries of the valleys are no longer working, whereas the towns of the North Wales coast are largely given over to tourism. The southern countryside has a beauty all its own, with two national parks and large areas are unspoiled and sometimes unvisited - but for the most part it lacks the sustained savagery of the mountains of Snowdonia.

Much of the south I would be exploring on this walk would be new to me. I knew something of the borders and had walked along the Pembrokeshire coast, but had seen little of the intervening hundred and fifty miles, which would be for the most part farming country with few villages and few people. Before reaching Wales, however I had the River Severn and the Forest of Dean to cross.

Central Gloucester, to which I returned on Saturday May 30th after my week at home looked no more appealing than it had on a Sunday. So, deciding I was not prepared to walk the three miles through city streets to reach the Severn Bridge, I found the bus station where a bus was just leaving for Minsterworth. At the cost of ninety pence it set me down outside the city boundary at the Apple Tree Inn.

I walked along to Church Lane and down to the churchyard of St Peter's right on the banks of the river. I went through double wrought-iron gates, built no doubt for access to the church from the river, and on to the Gloucestershire Way,

which follows the river at this point. I looked across open fields eastward to the ridge of the Cotswolds and westward to a dark mass of trees which could only be the Forest of Dean where I would be heading tomorrow. If I had but known it, there was a path to my B&B, Severn Bank, a little further along, but instead I walked back to the main road and entered the house drive the 'proper' way.

Severn Bank is a gracious building, Victorian I guessed, with its facade looking down an avenue of trees to the river, perhaps a quarter mile away. Minsterworth, I learned, was a good place for observers of the Severn Bore, a sort of tidal wave, created by irregularities in the river bed and the conflicting pressures of spring tides against descending land water. The Bore has a local Inn named after it, and its dates and times are published annually. Besides visiting to view the phenomenon, people come to ride the Severn Bore, but this weekend wasn't one of its times. If it had been, I don't think there would have been room for me to stay at Minsterworth.

My bedroom was huge with choice of single or double bed, easy chairs, its own bathroom and fresh milk to go with my tea. From my window I could see the river and the Cotswolds beyond, with showers sweeping over. The unsettled weather which had begun during my break was set to continue. Needing to get back into routine, I ate my own provisions and went early to bed.

Breakfast next morning was of the continental kind, with yogurt, different kinds of bread, cereals, ham and cheese, more to my liking than the full English breakfast more common in B&Bs. The couple sharing the breakfast room -

from Zimbabwe I learned - seemed disinclined for conversation and soon departed. But Mrs Carter came to talk and disclosed that she was looking after the place for her daughter and son-in-law, who were away on holiday. They had quite recently redecorated and modernised the house, keeping up with increasing demand for 'en suite' accommodation by installing showers in all the rooms. I left taking a generous packed lunch with me and with the weather clearing after overnight rain.

I went by the river for a while, along a path rather over-furnished with stiles, came back to cross the main A48 road, and headed west along another network of country lanes - farm tracks really. The hawthorn was fading and so was the cow-parsley, and the first fresh green of the trees had matured to the duller tones of summer, but forget-me-nots, wild roses and honeysuckle were coming into bloom in the hedgerows, and the air was full of the distinctive scent of elderflower. This was sparsely inhabited country, just the occasional farm, having little to disturb the peace, except the cuckoo, which was in full voice.

As seemed to be the norm for this walk, I had trouble with accommodation. Needing to go to Cinderford on the outskirts of the Forest of Dean, I had not found anywhere to stay. The person I spoke to at the Littledean Hotel said they would be recovering from a large party on Saturday night and wouldn't be ready for visitors on Sunday. I failed to raise any of the other numbers on my list, so booked at a farm at Longhope, which I rapidly found to be in the wrong direction: too far north and with only a main road as a route to Coleford for the following day. I decided that come what may, I must go to Cinderford, and hope for the best. The farmer's wife I spoke to at Longhope didn't sound too pleased at my cancelling the bed, but agreed that they weren't exactly on my route.

The countryside was changing; from the low-lying river plain I was coming into woods and parkland, and there were steep-sided wooded hills ahead. I climbed one of these, Pope's Hill, a long long way, to find myself rewarded with a dramatic view of the river making a huge S-shaped bend laid out as on a map. It was a sight to restore my morale, which had been flagging in anticipation of a long search for a bed for the night.

I found another telephone box, and made a last attempt to raise the Belfry, the only remaining number on my list, and in the way such things happen finally succeeded in booking a bed. The mile walk to Littledean, on the outskirts of Cinderford, was along the main road, narrow in places and uncomfortably busy with Sunday afternoon traffic. No sign of a pavement of course until I came into the village.

The Belfry was up a hill, a largish and noisy pub but my room was in a little outside annexe with its own bath and TV, and with a fine view of a hillside scattered with pretty cottages. What's more, the Spa grocery a few doors away was open and I was able to buy provisions and a Sunday paper. The day had turned out better than I'd feared.

The night had been so quiet that I was surprised next morning to find other residents at breakfast, business people mostly. Leaving, I found myself confronted with a mile climb up another steep hill. I was entering the Forest of Dean, one of England's largest ancient forests, occupying a wedge-shaped area of land between the rivers Severn and Wye. Cinderford, on the eastern flank of the forest, owes its name to the local abundance of iron and coal slag, having long been the centre of the forest's coal-mining industry. Notwithstanding its importance over centuries for iron and steel production and as a source of timber, the forest has attractions for visitors in its wild-life and wild flowers and can be explored by its many paths and trails.

I reached the summit of the hill at 237 metres and was given a clue to the prospect ahead in a house name: *Brecon View* it said. Sure enough, to the north-west was a new blue line, rapidly becoming obscured by grey, but undoubtedly the Brecon Beacons. Below was the dark mass of trees seen earlier from Severn Bank.

No sooner had I set foot in the Forest of Dean than the rain began; no more than a threat at first, but soon penetrating the tree cover and I prepared myself for a wet walk, with no shelter before Coleford. The forest looked majestic and splendid, with its mixture of ancient trees - oak, beech and conifers and carpets of wild flowers - which would repay exploration, but not today. I stayed close to the line of the road.

The disused mine at Cannop 'Open to Visitors' had a sign saying *cafe open*, but someone had forgotten either to open the cafe or to remove the sign and everywhere was firmly shut. By now the rain had turned into a deluge, with which even my Goretex jacket had difficulty in coping. I crept rather unhappily into Coleford, where I warmed up at Muffins restaurant with hot soup.

Like Cinderford, Coleford has an industrial history, of charcoal production and iron smelting, but is now just a small market town. I trawled its streets looking for somewhere to stay, and noticed that a goodly number of the shops and businesses bore the name Toombs, one of the several spellings of our name.

The two addresses on my list had no vacancies, surprisingly in a place lacking much in the way of tourist attractions. Anyway, I went to the tourist information centre, always a good resource if you happen to be there at the right time of day. The helpful young man there rang round and found me a bed at the Forest Hotel, which was only a hundred yards up the road. This was a no-frills commercial hotel, but perfectly adequate, and the proprietor told me that the building had once been occupied by a Toombs, which made me wonder if there was any past family connection. I had a hot bath, went shopping and bought fish and chips for supper.

Heard at breakfast: 'But we can't go anywhere without the car'. *O tempora, O mores.*

The night had been stormy with lashing wind and rain, and the forecast was of more to come. I bought a roll and bananas from the nice man at the greengrocers and went on a quiet little road over the hill 'unsuitable for caravans'. There were different flowers in the verges: marguerites, clover, foxgloves, and pink and white morning glory climbing the hedges. The landscape was contorted - great lumps of wooded hills forcing the road into loops around their flanks.

I descended along the banks of a swiftly-flowing stream into the Wye valley near Redbrook and found a road sign

GWENT

Pencelli
Crickhowell
Llanfihangel Crucorney
Penclawydd
Great Trehiw
Offa's Dyke
White Castle
Monmouth
A40
Monmouth & Brecon Canal

Monmouth to Pencelli

telling me I was in Merionnydd. Over the border I went and found a footpath by the river following the road into Monmouth, waymarked if overgrown. Two miles later I rejoined the road, to see across it the familiar sight of the Kymin. This is National Trust property, a hill with a naval temple on top, built in 1800 to perpetuate the names of some of the distinguished admirals of the late eighteenth century. The Kymin is one of the landmarks on the Offa's Dyke path.

I crossed a bridge and had my first real encounter with the A40, a dual carriageway cutting me off from the streets of Monmouth, which was only accessible by a dreary underpass.

Monmouth as I remembered the town was changed out of all recognition since my last visit, which must have been eighteen years ago. Although the A40 did its best to bypass the town, its narrow streets were still clogged with heavy traffic from the north and only a small paved area protected pedestrians. It felt hazardous to cross the road. I walked through town to inspect the Monnow bridge, with its fortified gatehouse and phoned Dick, who sounded as harassed as I felt. I laid in supplies at the brand new Waitrose, had coffee and a toasted sandwich, and visited the tourist information in the rather grand Town Hall to book the next night's bed. I had to let myself in for rather more mileage than I'd wanted for tomorrow - the helpful assistant knew the farmer's wife and said I'd be well looked after.

My B&B for this night was a half-mile outside the town, a nice-looking stone house set on a hillside. I was shown into a cell-like room, which had a bed, a wash-basin, a cupboard, and a view across the valley to the A40! And to my dismay, no tea-making facilities, which I'd increasingly come to regard as a necessity. I asked my hostess if there was a room where I could watch the weather forecast, a coded request for somewhere more comfortable to spend the evening. My request was curtly refused: 'The weather forecast is never right for here anyway.' Definitely Category One, where priorities obviously didn't include fraternising with guests. At least I had a fine view of the Kymin, with a marvellous cloudscape, and found a Ruth Rendell thriller to read.

The good news is, I wrote in my journal, *that I'm not much more than a hundred and fifty miles away from St David's.*

Next morning I re-crossed the Monnow bridge and came to an Offa's Dyke path waymark just as the rain was starting. The path is another national trail, about a hundred and eighty miles in length, reaching coast to coast from Chepstow on the Bristol Channel to Prestatyn on the Irish Sea. It follows the course of the earthwork built along the England-Wales border by Offa, King of Mercia in the eighth century. It is a varied route, crossing the Black Mountains of South Wales in its early stages and the northern Clwydian Hills before descending to the sea. I had walked Offa's Dyke with Dick one early spring wearing some discarded boots which had been outgrown by our son Robert; these cast-offs wreaked havoc on my heels and toes - the only time I have ever suffered from blisters and a lesson to me to wear my own boots!

I left Offa's Dyke path in favour of a route along minor roads to its west, leaving behind the racket of the A40 and within a mile, to my great relief, finding myself on a different map. I had grown heartily sick of looking at the Gloucester one. The new map heralded changes in the countryside, which became friendlier, its dimensions more suited to humans than the austere and sterile agribusiness of East Anglia and the Home Counties. The lanes were lined with the kinds of hedges long disappeared from East Anglia and black and white Friesian cows grazed in the fields - and of course there were sheep. I found a baby chaffinch sitting in the middle of the road not wanting to move for me; a red kite hovered and swooped.

I climbed on and on and on and reached a long ridge and triangulation point where the view opened up. With excitement I recognised more hills, the weird shape of the Skirrid (Ysgyryd in Welsh) and the Hatteral Ridge of the Black Mountains where the Offa's Dyke path would go. The rain had stopped and I was seeing a landscape probably fifteen miles distant. I joined the Offa's Dyke path and immediately met two walkers coming south, only two stages from the end of their ten-day walk, so we stopped for the usual exchange of greetings.

Wearying, I went through Llantilio Crossenny, where the Hostry Inn was firmly shut, and started another long climb up and up to White Castle, one of three built by the Normans in the twelfth century to secure their borders. From the summit there was a view of the Skirrid dominant to the west and now much nearer. I did a long descent to the road and found with relief the farm track to Great Trehiw.

As promised by the lady in the Information Centre, my reception couldn't have been more different from that of the previous night. I was shown to a large room with double bed and a view over green fields and hills with sheep grazing. Anne Beavans apologised for not being able to provide a 'proper' evening meal. Unusually, she said, she was going out but there was soup and bread - a whole crusty loaf - and cheese and salad, and I had the run of the small kitchen and comfortable sitting room. While I was eating two fellow guests appeared; they had been doing the Three Castles Walk, a local trail visiting Skenfrith, Grosmont and White Castles. It's a nineteen-mile walk, and, taking into account the number of hills to climb, a tough day's outing. They went off quickly for dinner at the Walnut Tree Inn, a local hostelry with a national reputation.

I looked out later on the same hillside; with the advancing summer and my steady westward progress, the evenings were becoming longer, and there was still some light in the sky. The landscape was picked out in shades of grey, like a Chinese painting, and the sheep were asleep, motionless, and making no sound. It was impossible in the dusk to distinguish them from the few rounded rocks in the field. Did sheep, I wondered count humans to help them sleep? I had always thought of sheep as being restless, even neurotic; after all, for many of them their lives are at the mercy of humans from birth until they reach the dinner plate, so they can hardly be expected not to show symptoms of anxiety. This vista of tranquillity was so unutterably calming that it was difficult to imagine that other world of aggressive activity and noise that I'd left just over the hill in Monmouth. I slept as if the A40 and everything associated with it didn't exist.

Next morning Ann Beavans telephoned 'down the line' to her friend Anne Davies at Pen Clawdd, and sent me off with a bacon sandwich and all sorts of good wishes.

After yesterday's rain the air was soft and warm. I waited in Llangattock Lingoed for the pub to open for coffee, then climbed on to another ridge, with the Black Mountains now dominating the view over the valley of the River Monnow. A car passed, stopped, reversed and the driver, an American with his wife, asked if I wouldn't consider cheating for a few miles - they'd like to offer me a lift. I had to refuse gracefully; it was a fine day, I had plenty of time and I'd done more than enough cheating already.

I crossed the A485 trunk road and came into the village of Llanvihangel Crucorney, reflecting on the euphony of Welsh placenames. There is another famous inn here, the Skirrid Mountain Inn, which dates back to AD1110 when the village was on a trading route from Hereford, and, notoriously, Judge Jeffreys pronounced sentence from a courtroom in the inn. I bought a can of drink from a churlish shopkeeper, and discovered that the garage two doors away was also selling provisions, so that perhaps accounted for his ill-humour.

I climbed out of the village and found the drive to Pen Clawdd. There was an imposing building with a gabled roof about a half mile away up the drive but the farm was much closer, a modern building. Anne Davies welcomed me hospitably and offered tea and fruit cake in the garden, where I spent the rest of the afternoon writing postcards. The building up the drive, I learned, was a prestigious hotel, not widely advertised because exclusive, and was in demand by television companies for their more up-market productions.

The area had been in the news when Janet Street Porter had visited it on her long walk fron Dungeness to Conwy, a more ambitious project then mine. Janet had followed the course of the Cambrian Way, which takes a high level route from south to north Wales.

Anne Davies bade me a warm farewell, saying she would be thinking of me constantly over the coming weeks and I left with the feeling of being valued that only such encounters can give. Aiming to avoid more contact with the A40 in Abergavenny, I intended to make my way through the quiet lanes behind the Sugar Loaf Mountain.

I followed the road into the Honddhu valley, which leads to Llanthony in the heart of the Black Mountains. Llanthony is the site of a twelfth-century priory in a beautiful setting of meadows and chestnut groves, and is much visited for its history and association with St David who, it is said, ate here the leeks which were to become the Welsh badge. I have to admit that I prefer daffodils as an emblem. I would have to defer a visit to Llanthony until another day, since it wasn't really on my route.

After a mile I took a road signed to Forest Coal Pit, just a single track weaving its way round the hillside and climbing high above the Grwyne river. The road crossed a swampy area, long green grasses and reeds concealing a multitude of wetland plants, mallow, asphodel and marsh marigolds and a plant I hadn't met before, but later identified as bistort or snake-root, having small candle-like lilac flowers.

Further along the road I came to Pant nature reserve, with a board walk nature trail among the trees. There followed a long long descent to Crickhowell, one of those where you look down on rooftops and wish you had wings. This small Welsh town, alas, has the A40 for its main street, but also possesses a river and a castle and some old houses and people go there for hang-gliding. I found a small cafe where I had coffee and a Welsh cake, then, still feeling hungry, bought fish and chips and ate them in the recreation ground near the ruined castle.

Later I wrote in my diary *If variety is the spice of life I'm thoroughly spiced!* I had found only one B&B address in Crickhowell and this turned out to be as close to the A40 as you could get, only a few yards separating the house from the ever-present traffic. A greater contrast to the previous two nights' blissful peace could not be imagined. Surprisingly, I slept.

Next day, Saturday, I was to be a gongoozler. The word doesn't appear in Chambers' dictionary, but was invented during the construction of the canals in the eighteenth century. A gongoozler was someone who took no part in the work, but hung around taking a critical look at the proceedings. Nowadays I understand the word to be descriptive of someone to be met on canal banks having nothing better to do, unlike those who travel along the canal by long-boat or kayak or sit by it with fishing rods. A gongoozler will hang around the locks waiting for someone to fall in. I was just going to walk along a few miles of the Monmouthshire and Brecon canal, but suspected that a walker would have the status of gongoozler.

I walked through Crickhowell, busy with Saturday morning traffic and crossed fields to reach the canal bank. I would follow the canal to Pencelli, where I had arranged to meet my daughter Caroline.

This was familiar country. I have fond memories of an idyllic week spent in Brecon in 1989, where the canal had been on the route of a long challenge walk which required an ascent of the Brecon Beacons and Black Mountains. We had stayed in a converted milking parlour near the canal and in heat-wave conditions had walked out parts of the route.

The Monmouthshire and Brecon is a scenic canal, built along the hillside above the valley of the Usk River, thus giving a fine view over the surrounding countryside. Work has been done to make an easy walking surface and to maintain access for vessels, and there is a virtual absence of time-consuming locks. The trouble, however, with canal walks, is that there are limits to how much the scenery can be varied; on the one hand is the water, with none of the small cataracts and flurries found in rivers, and on the other the banks, usually tree-girt. No stiles to climb, an imperceptible gradient. The only distraction on this stretch was the occasional bridge or the passing longboat. It was as if one section of path was rolled up behind me and laid out again in front, looking exactly as before, so that I had no sensation of onward progress.

It was a relief to arrive at Tal y Bont on Usk, where a coffee shop had opened since my last visit. There was a swing bridge with a notice to water travellers *Please do not open during times of travel to school* and a group of youngsters was heaving canoes up the canal bank. There were plenty of gongoozlers here, feeding the waterfowl or hanging around in true gongoozling fashion.

I had coffee and a toasted teacake, and walked on to Pencelli, where I booked in at Cambrian Cruisers, a farmhouse on the banks of the canal which also housed the business of a marina, although with none of the bustle of Tal y Bont.

While I was in the bath Caroline with partner Andy arrived, having driven from Nottingham. With a fine sense of priorities, having accompanied me on a previous walk, Caroline had brought a plentiful supply of delicious food, fruit and cakes and other goodies, so we had a feast while catching up on each other's news.

My room had a mountain view of the Brecon Beacons, with showers chasing each other over their summits, and I discovered that I had walked on to yet another map. Tomorrow would be a short day with Caroline as my escort.

Chapter 10

Not the Little Chef

The Brecon Beacons National Park boasts four groups of hills, of which the best known and most visited for their hill-walking are the Brecon Beacons. This group of summits, while none reaches the magical three thousand foot height, still are subject to changing conditions and weather so are a worthy challenge to hill-walkers. Because of their isolation from other mountain masses they provide wonderful view-points.

Caroline and I planned to walk to Libanus at the north-western limit of the Beacons, a route which would take us over their lower slopes, although missing the best views. From Libanus I would be aiming for central South Wales through Llandovery and Carmarthen, which was all new country to me.

Caroline and Andy had stayed overnight at a B&B in Tal y Bont, and were back at Cambrian Cruisers for an early getaway. Andy would drive to Libanus where he would wait for our arrival on foot. The morning wasn't too promising, with clouds spilling over the Beacons but looked like improving. We set off along another mile of canal, soon to come within earshot of the A40 as it took a wide sweep around Brecon. We found a sequence of lanes which took us high into the outliers of the Beacons, with the short showers barely wetting us, meeting few people, just a cavalcade on horseback and a group of four on a Duke of Edinburgh award scheme coming from the summit of Pen y Fan, the high point of the Beacons.

There was a long descent to the Tai'r Bull hotel whose white buildings were visible below long before we reached the main road, and Andy was waiting in the comfortable bar with the Sunday papers. Our afternoon was spent in a reconnaissance drive: I needed to find somewhere to stay on Monday night, when I would be in Trecastle on the A40. We didn't have much success; the motel marked on the map was derelict, and there was no sign of Login House where I had stayed in 1989. In the end I booked myself in at the Tai'r Bull for Sunday night and resigned myself to paying more than I'd wanted at the Castle Coaching Inn at Trecastle on Monday.

The Tai'r Bull was cheaper and a friendly place offering another view of the Beacons, giving, I feared, the threat of bad weather. I waved off Caroline and Andy on their journey to Nottingham and spent a peaceful evening.

Next morning I climbed steeply out of Libanus into woods, passed a mountain centre, and joined a Roman Road on open moorland. A strong wind was blowing and ragged clouds chased each other across a rapidly darkening sky, and sure enough the rain started when I was on the high point of the road at over a thousand feet, the Brecon Beacons now totally obscured. This was wild exposed country lacking in shelter of any kind and I thought the Romans couldn't have enjoyed it much.

I walked down the road into Sennybridge with the rain intensifying and looked for shelter and food. There was a fish and chip shop, *Closed on Mondays* and nothing much else. I realised I was back on the A40, and walked along it for a half-mile, wondering if it might boast a Little Chef.

Sure enough, I crossed a bridge and turned a corner to see across the road just the place, a 'not the Little Chef' but its equivalent, a roadside cafe next to a petrol station. A group of four bedraggled touring cyclists were just leaving. I had egg and chips and a big mug of coffee and dried off, but there was no sign of any clearance by the time I'd finished so it was back on with waterproofs, and a wet walk over the back roads to Trecastle, which was only three miles distant.

The Castle Inn was nice, a seventeenth-century building once used as a stage coach halt on the road from Gloucester to Llandovery. Now it is a family-run concern, and gave a warm welcome to one weatherworn walker. I was shown to a huge room with equally large bathroom and draped wet clothes over all, then ate vegetarian lasagne in the comfortable bar, realising that my fellow guests were all non-English speaking.

A blissfully comfortable night, worth the day's wetting. Continental breakfast was imaginatively good: yogurt, fresh fruit, freshly baked breads and rolls, and a new-laid perfectly boiled egg.

I had a warm send-off from the Castle into still wild and wet conditions. I had planned to join the Roman road heading west-and-north-westward from Brecon, crossing high ground to the south of the valley carrying the A40. The track reaches a high camp, at y Pigwyn, where there are even older fortifications. This may be an extension of Sarn Helen, a long road reaching from Caernarvon in the north to

Carmarthen in the south, which Welsh traditional legend says was made by the Roman Governor at the request of his wife Helen. The more prosaic probability is that the road linked up a series of forts along its line as a means of controlling the rebellious Celts.

The clouds were low over the hills and I didn't much fancy the idea of climbing into them and getting wet again. The unattractive alternative was to walk ten miles along the A40 to Llandovery, following the route of the stage-coaches of earlier years. This seemed like taking my life in my hands, but in the end that's what I decided to do.

Outside the village the road was level and littered with large black slugs; thereafter it climbed into trees giving little harbour to pedestrians on its many bends, but with scant traffic was just about tolerable. For the most part the road followed the course of the river Gwyderrig, which would at Llandovery join the larger Tywi, flowing along the wide valley down to Carmarthen.

The road took a sweeping bend and a bright blue road-sign announced the place-name Halfway. This village once possessed three inns and was an important stop on the drove road and later stage-coach route between Milford on the Pembroke coast and Gloucester. It is twenty-two years since the last pub closed, and only one house is occupied now, the remainder having fallen victim to road-widening or other aspects of development. The post-office, still with its post-box showing collection times, is also derelict.

Further along the road I came to a lay-by, more a refuge and stopped for my mid-morning banana. An obelisk recorded the fate of coach-driver Edward Jenkins in 1835 who, intoxicated, lost control of the Gloucester-Carmarthen coach and precipitated coach and passengers thirty-one feet down the steep hillside and into the river. The obelisk was erected as a warning to other road-users, surely an early instance of a drink-driving accident? Even today the sharp elbow curve in the road requires care.

I was in Llandovery by early afternoon with the rain easing, another nice old town bearing evidence of its coaching history in old inns and a fine cobbled market place with small interesting shops. George Borrow, another celebrated long distance walker, stayed here on his journey through Wild Wales in 1862 and described it as 'the pleasantest ...halt in the course of all my wanderings'.

I went in search of food and drink and once again dried out, already feeling I was being presented with too much wet Welsh weather and hoping that this wasn't becoming habitual. I visited the tourist office to do more research on mid-Wales accommodation. The next day Dick was joining me again and I could see I was going to have trouble once more.

I walked down a long road past the station and came to the road bridge over the Tywi, which here was fast-flowing and deep, swollen by the recent rains, the kind of river that invites you to stay and look. Just over the bridge was my B&B for the night, Llwyncelyn Guest House and, would you believe it, by the side of the A40 but sufficiently removed from it to ensure some peace and quiet. In its defence I have to say that by now the A40 had calmed down somewhat; like a country road it wound on into the trees as it left the town boundary, with traffic down to a trickle.

That evening I reviewed progress and found I was less than a hundred miles from St David's, which would make me about ten days' walk from my destination. It came as a shock to find that I had moved on so far and fast, but if I wanted to extend the walk westward I would need to cross the sea to Ireland, a possibility I had once considered but rejected.

As I went back over the level crossing next morning, a well-dressed gentleman stopped and asked where I was going. To Llangadog, I said. 'I can show you a short cut by the river,' said he, 'and my wife would like to give you coffee.' I had to refuse; once again I needed to shop, and there would be nowhere after Llandovery - but I went on feeling rather ungracious.

It was only six miles to Cynyll (Knish) Farm, where I was to meet Dick, driving up from London. The countryside had changed. I had left the Brecon hills behind, and was walking across a broad open farming landscape, fields reaching down to the river and lower wooded hills on either side. The A40 was now on the far side of the river, its sound barely audible.

I turned down a narrow farm track which crossed a small stream, then climbed a hill. At its summit I stopped to look at the view of a ridge of hills to the south-east, which I identified as the Black Mountain, the last and the most remote of the ranges of the Brecon hills before the land declines towards the coast. I found the drive to Cynyll Farm a quarter mile further along the road, with Friesian cattle in the fields.

Jackie and Terry were at lunch but at once offered tea and cakes. I settled in and walked back up the road, soon to see the familiar sight of our yellow motor caravan coming along. I persuaded Dick to walk back up the hill with me to see the view before guiding him to the farm. This was a comfortable homely place, accepting guests as part of the life of the farm, and Jackie's cooking made the meals something special. Her desserts were particularly good, with home-made ice-cream of a flavour never found in supermarket offerings.

I had booked us in for two nights. I had been walking for twelve days since Gloucester and although the walking had not been arduous I felt the need to stay in one place just for one day. When I said this to Dick he objected: 'But what shall we do all day?' Ha! I didn't think time would hang heavily on our hands. We had to plan a route, search yet again for places to stay, and shop for provisions.

And so it proved. We first drove into Llandovery, for which I had begun to feel an affection. We parked in the shadow of the medieval castle on its mound, revisited the tourist office, and shopped. Our researches for accommodation for the weekend were less than successful, and finally we went on a tour of the country ahead looking for those elusive B&B signs, driving into a remote network of precipitous lanes where we soon expected to be walking. Partially succeeding, we had a picnic lunch on a high point overlooking the Tywi valley and so managed to fill in the greater part of the day.

Leaving our vehicle parked in the farmyard, where it looked thoroughly at home beside tractors and a milk bowser, we set off next morning on foot, waved off by Jackie and Terry, and their other guest Barry, and observed by their two cats and an importunate puppy, a sheepdog trainee, said Terry. This would be the final stage of my journey. In not much more than a week I should be in St David's.

Llangadog to Trebersed

DYFED

Llangadog
River Tywi
A40
Capel Isaac
Pant Gwyn
River Tywi
A40
Afon Cothi
CARMARTHEN
Trebersed

Chapter 11

On the roller-coaster

And when you need to rest and eat
Let's hope you find a pleasant seat

Lesley Dunn

We walked down the hill into the village of Llangadog - just one terrace of houses and a milk processing factory. There is a station here too, on the line of the mid-Wales railway, a scenic route which from Swansea threads its way through the centre of some of the most remote and beautiful country of mid-Wales, to end its journey at Shrewsbury. By some miracle this line survived the cuts of the sixties and now thrives as a tourist route. We went over the level crossing, crossed a river, Afon Bran, and reached the A40. We crossed this too, and started along a narrow lane uphill, 'Into Indian country,' I said.

I'd better say something about how we proposed to get to St David's Head, which was by this time about eighty miles due west of us. One thing I'd realised quite early on was that once I was away from the well-trodden paths there would be no clear walkers' route which avoided roads. On the other hand, the countryside north of the A40 is little visited. It is a complex landscape, not spectacular in the way that large mountains are, or wild like the Pennine moorlands, or open like the Ridgeway. It is a secret country, closed and introverted, and we found that only on going into it could we appreciate its qualities, unlike, say the Brecon Beacons, whose silhouette is unmistakable, and which dominate the view of the approaching traveller.

This secretive element may be due to the geography of the area. It is dissected by rivers arising in the hilly mid-Wales uplands and flowing south. There are many of these watercourses in the path of the west-bound traveller, not large, but with steep-sided, sometimes precipitous banks. Travel across the grain of this country is therefore akin to a ride on a roller coaster. The way ahead is not always obvious, the walker finding the few places where bridges exist, always following steep descents, and with equally steep climbs thereafter, on to a plateau or ridge, to be rewarded with views of little-known landscapes. The countryside is of rich farmland, with large areas of woodland crowning its hills, and the few villages seem to be on the road to nowhere; it is rare to find pub or shop, although each small community has its chapel.

The map didn't give us much help in showing any public rights of way to speak of going in our direction, but there was an equivalent dearth of any main roads. The network of small farm roads, however, promised steady progress largely untroubled by traffic or the prospect of encounters with towns of any size short of St David's itself.

On this question of rights of way, the Countryside Commission some years ago set a target for local authorities of the opening up of all rights of way in England and Wales by the year 2000; a target which seems less and less achievable as the millenium approaches. In Wales, for example, it is said that a walker setting out on a public right of way has a less than one in twenty chance of completing it unobstructed over a distance of two miles or more. Results of a recent survey show that more than 4,000 miles of Welsh rights of way are 'unusable or can only be used with great difficulty'. This is not necessarily because of deliberate obstruction of routes, but paths which are little used and not maintained rapidly become difficult of access. In my home walking areas of Kent and Surrey there are many willing volunteers who take upon themselves the tasks of keeping paths open, but I imagine that there may be just too few people able to undertake the task in the remote areas we were approaching.

Today we were heading for our first river crossing, of the Afon Dulais, engaging in a routine which was to become familiar. This entailed beginning with a climb on to a ridge at a height of about five hundred feet with views northward into the central hills.

We were in red kite country, which was for many years the last remaining breeding place in Wales of this spectacular bird of prey. The red kite went into decline partly because of changes in habitat and farming practice, and partly because it used to be hunted or worse, poisoned, by farmers and keepers, being blamed, sometimes unjustly, for attacks on livestock. Nowadays red kites have a protected status and their numbers have increased above the danger level. They are attractive birds, distinguished by their reddish-brown colour, forked tails and method of flight. 'It seems to have taught us the art of steering,' said one observer, speaking of the way the bird uses its tail as a rudder.

There was a longer climb up from the river, through the woods of Taliaris estate. A mound in a field marked the prehistoric settlement Maes y Castell, and ahead a pair of red kites flew almost into our faces from a rocky bluff. Somewhere below on our left was the valley carrying A40 road, railway and the river Twyi, not far in distance but seeming a world away in its pace of life. We followed the road along the ridge and came upon the scattered houses of Capel Isaac, where we were to spend the night.

The Manse was down a little side road, and here we met yet another Mr Smith and his Vietnamese wife. Mr Smith had two new knee replacements and was on crutches but still managed to climb a ladder to repair his roof, damaged in recent storms, and to work on his smallholding, which was described as organic. 'Fur and feathers,' read the Tourist Board's publicity leaflet. Mr Smith also makes his own wines, and presented us with a bottle to go with our dinner. The decor was oriental in character, with many red-shaded lamps, and every surface held all kinds of elaborate ornaments.

What we chiefly remember about the Manse, however, is how cold we felt there, in an unheated house on a distinctly chilly June evening, with rain threatening. We sat through dinner wearing outdoor clothes and retired to bed to keep warm soon afterwards.

Morning brought the promised rain, clouds low on the hillside. Today we were on the roller-coaster in earnest, with four river-valleys to cross, of which the largest was the Afon Cothi. I knew about the Cothi from a past visit to the central

Welsh hills, when we had stayed at Pumsaint near the site of the Roman gold mine at Dolaucothi. George Borrow had stayed in the Dolau Cothi Arms in Pumsaint, and so had Edward Thomas, where he wrote the introduction to his Icknield Way book. I would have liked to revisit Pumsaint, but it was well off route.

There were first the Afon Dulas and the Afon Sannan to cross, each in its secluded tree-girt valley. As we walked down the approach to the Afon Cothi the rain set in in earnest as only Welsh rain can. The Cothi was in spate, an impressive and scenic river, rushing between rocky banks with flooded verges. We came to the crossing, which turned out to be a wartime design Bailey Bridge, with ruined pillars showing where the original crossing had been. Just a few houses and a telephone box graced its opposite bank, and the road climbed into the trees ahead. At the top of the hill we met an old man cutting the grass verge with an old-fashioned long-handled scythe, looking like Father Time himself. He'd lived in Capel Isaac 'as a boy', he told us.

The rain eased off for a while, then came on even more enthusiastically as we approached the B road going to Carmarthen, with a clap of thunder for good measure. Hard by the junction was a seat, and I sank on to it gratefully, feeling worn out from the morning's exertions and heedless of the rain. Dick, however, in his habitually resourceful fashion, wasted no time in looking for shelter, finding it in some kind of builder's yard behind a house opposite. In the yard was a sort of open-fronted hovel, with washing lines strung across it hung with old carpets leaving us just enough room to creep in and huddle in acute discomfort while the storm passed. A workman looked on sympathetically and offered us a lift; he wasn't going in our direction, which was fortunate for our determination to continue on foot.

The rain stopped and unexpectedly the sun came out so we went back to the friendly seat and ate our lunch. Things improved; we walked for a mile along the B road, our first sighting of anything like a major thoroughfare since Llangadog, then turned off to follow the course of the Afon Annell, this time flowing gently along a wide valley. We crossed the river and climbed another super-steep hill, to arrive at Pant Gwyn, which advertised itself as a farm guesthouse. This was luxury compared with the spartan Manse; the central heating was fully on, we were given cake with our tea, and wallowed in hot baths, then ate a gourmet meal.

Dick, after twice hitting his head, had noticed that the blackened oak beams in our room did not appear to be supporting the ceiling, and at breakfast asked Tim Giles, who runs the guesthouse, why this was. Tim replied that 'You're the first guest in nine years to have asked that question.'

'How many guests would that be?' I asked. Almost three thousand a year was the answer.

The beams, he said, had supported the roof of the sixteenth-century farmhouse, and the ceiling had been raised when extensive conversion works had been carried out much later, leaving few traces of the original building.

We had decided rather reluctantly that we would have to go through the town of Carmarthen on our next stage, partly because of the need to find a bridge over the river Gwili and partly to find a food shop (this would be the first since leaving Llandovery). On the way we were looking carefully at the doors of houses and barns on the few farmhouses we passed. Tim had said that traditionally these were painted red as a way of warding off evil spirits, a custom which was still carried on even although the reason might have been forgotten. We observed that indeed the predominant colour of the paintwork was red; no greens, blues or browns.

The little lane we took funnelled us eventually on to a real main road, where some prodigious road works were in progress, but pedestrians were well catered for by specially made footways. We found a footpath which took us around the back of the hospital, crossed the A40 and climbed above the Twyi river on yet another path which brought us out on the outskirts of Carmarthen.

The A40 gives Carmarthen a wide berth, leaving the town centre marooned within a circle of main roads. The town was quiet and we walked on with little hope of finding shops open on a Sunday, but a helpful passer-by directed us into a pedestrianised area with a statue of a local dignitary in its centre. Here we warmed up in a fish restaurant with fishcakes and chips, then found just along the road an open Co-op.

Our destination for the evening, Trebersed Farm, was two miles outside Carmarthen, a rather dreary walk between suburban houses at first. Once back on a country road we looked for the track shown on our map as leading over the hillside to the farm, but were dismayed to discover a gate with a rude keep out notice and the warning *Loose dogs.* Uncertain if this was our route we knocked at the door of a cottage a few yards away. A large man came to the door clad only in the scantiest of towels. We had a confused conversation about the location of Trebersed, which at first we were assured was in the opposite direction from the placename clearly marked on our map, but finally our informant agreed that we could reach the farm 'just through the woods and over the hill', and we should disregard the 'keep out' sign. The owner of the notice was a newcomer to the area and should be ignored.

And so it proved. We crept cautiously past another gate with barking dogs on its far side, past a car blocking our way, over two rickety stiles through a wood, and came out on to a green track with a fine view back over the town. To the south the land fell away to meet the A40, invisible from here, and we realised that not too far beyond it was the estuary of the Tywi river and the open sea.

We followed the track as it wound its way around the hillside, negotiated a wire fence, and came face to face with a half-dozen black and white cows placidly making their way back to the field from the milking shed. There was no one to escort them - it seemed as if they had come this way all their lives and needed no human direction. We stopped to let them by, then went through gates into the farmyard.

Ahead was the farmhouse, a neat white building within a rectangle of outbuildings with a solar panel on its roof and bright summer flowers in its small garden, looking like a child's picture of a farm. In a few minutes we came to the door where we were warmly welcomed with tea. Rosemary, our hostess, had just returned from a rally of the Countryside Alliance in Cardiff; there was to be a summit meeting there of the European Community's Agricultural ministers, and the farmers wanted to raise awareness of their problems.

I knew about the Countryside Alliance of course. It had been given massive publicity by the rally of a quarter of a million farmers and their workers, landowners, and country dwellers in general in Hyde Park in London earlier in the year. Like many city dwellers, however, I had thought of the rally as relating to landowners' opposition to the forthcoming Hunting with Dogs bill, and to Government plans to bring in legislation to create access to open spaces. The movement, I thought, was a last-ditch attempt by landowners to protect their own interests.

All this was, to some extent true; but while ordinary farmers were taking an active part in the Alliance's work it seemed that although their participation was sought and welcomed, all the publicity was given to more controversial issues while their real needs had been ignored. I hadn't realised and only fully appreciated in talking with Rosemary, and Tom, her husband, how desperate was the situation in which small hill farmers found themselves, where their very survival was in doubt. I have always enjoyed staying on farms, where there is peace and quiet rarely found in our overcrowded towns and cities. Farm dwellers are generous in sharing their homes with townspeople, but we can enjoy the countryside for a few days and go back to our secure existence confident in the knowledge that these oases will be there for us another time. But it seems that we may not have that assurance for too much longer.

The outlook is particularly bleak for small hill farmers because, I learned, their livelihood is at risk through problems such as the collapse of livestock prices, the high pound, high interest rates. The large agribusinesses of East Anglia are in better shape, their operations are well subsidised, their profits are high, and they are better able to withstand economic setbacks. The people that we met were struggling to pay their day-to-day bills and interest on bank loans, let alone make a profit, although we could tell whenever we stayed at a farm that their work was a way of life which they enjoyed and would not want to give up. There is more than one side, I know, to the problems of the farming community, but in hearing personal stories of their plight I could not help but feel emotionally involved and knew that from then on I would see the countryside and its farms not simply as contributing to my pleasure but as fulfilling a vital role in preserving the features we love best about it. I am grateful for this learning, because it has changed a way of thinking.

I would think about Trebersed and farms like it as we went on towards St David's and would look with newly-opened eyes on signs of what was happening to the countryside. I just hope that the small hill farms of Wales survive.

Chapter 12

One more river...

*Roads go on
While we forget and are
Forgotten like a star
That shoots and is gone.*

Edward Thomas

The walk had by now acquired a momentum of its own, of the kind that I remembered from other long distance walks. It takes a while to acquire a rhythm which will persist over the miles, and I don't think I shall ever cease to feel a thrill when I find that things are going to plan and I am really going to reach my objective. In the case of this walk, I had been on the point of giving up more than once, brought near to defeat by practical problems which sometimes seemed insurmountable. But once past some point of no return such worries become irrelevant. I took it for granted that I should leave point A each morning and arrive at point B each evening and that nothing now was going to get in my way. There is a great freedom in having no other distractions like telephone calls or shopping to do or meals to cook or people to see; the fact of needing to concentrate only on this one task of reaching each day's objective simplifies life enormously and is the best aid to relaxation I know.

Preselli Hills

Afon Taf

Llanboidy

Ffynnonlwyd

Trebersed

A 40

A 478

Login

Nant-y-ffin motel

Eastern Cleddau River

Trebersed to Eastern Cleddau.

Knowing that this stage of the walk would involve the almost continuous use of roads I had been expecting to miss the challenge of finding my way across open country but soon began to find pleasure in this different kind of walking.

The lie of the land meant that there was constant variety in the changing scenery. We would climb from the secret hidden river valleys to the clean fresh air of the uplands where there was always something new to see: the multitude of flowers in the verges, the ever-present wildlife, and the distant views, now holding out the promise of our steady approach to the coast. An occasional farm tractor went by, otherwise it was a rare event to see a car except near the few sparsely spaced villages. I took it as a sign of the times that few of these cars were less than five years old, compared with almost universally newer ones in the more prosperous south-east.

Trying to put myself in the position of travellers of old and taking the path of least resistance I had drawn a line on the map which would take us almost due west (give a diversion or two for rivers) and along which we would travel to reach the city of St David's without first touching the Pembroke coast. The maps, showing ancient settlements and monuments, provided evidence that pilgrims travelling to St David's in other times might have journeyed this way, although I knew that the valley of the Twyi, now taking the west-bound traffic of the A40, had been a drove road along which had travelled earlier traders and those bound for ancient places of worship.

The weather was fine, something to be noted in observedly unsettled conditions; there were big blue patches and a brisk north-west wind. It was the same routine as before: a succession of steep climbs and descents marked by little black arrows on the map, to cross a sequence of small torrents: Cywin, Dewi, and Cynin. On reaching the first ridge we saw to the north another line of blue hills; these were the Preselli mountains, a mysterious range scattered with prehistoric sites and with connections to Stonehenge, whose inner circle is said to be derived from the blue stone to be found in these hills. We would march along the flanks of the Preselli hills until almost within sight of the coast.

It was a good day for walking along quiet lanes with the meadowsweet coming into bloom. We watched a buzzard hunting while drinking our coffee and ate lunch on one of those friendly seats in the children's playground at Meidrim. From Trebersed we had been 'passed down the line', and in the late afternoon we descended the farm road to Ffynnon Llywdd (White Fountain), just another small dairy farm of which Haydn and Eleri Lloyd were the third generation of occupiers. Eleri's mother and grandmother had both offered bed and breakfast accommodation here.

We had by now developed a sort of check list of the kinds of facilities on offer at the typical B&B, and a view of what we considered the priorities among them. First for us was the cup of tea on arrival, preferably served in the house sitting-room, but in any case having what is now called a 'hospitality tray' in our room. There followed things like hot bath-water, (bath not shower), blankets rather than duvets, enough coat-hangers, reading-lights which could be turned off from the bed, and a pub or fish and chip shop within easy walking distance. A TV set came rather low down the list, although I had sometimes appreciated one on a solo stay with no one to talk to and nothing to read. I had never, however, expected a jacuzzi to be on anyone's list, and until Ffynnon Llwydd had never even met one.

For the uninitiated, a jacuzzi is a device fitted in a bath-tub which sends out under-water jets to massage and invigorate the body. Possibly everyone offering accommodation to walkers should think of investing in one. With some trepidation I turned the switch to activate the device, and found it making noises as if it had acute indigestion, because I hadn't used enough water; the verdict was that a jacuzzi takes getting used to!

Haydn Lloyd had come from the milking to let us in, and we'd had tea and tested the jacuzzi by the time Eleri had returned from her job in St Clears. Eleri, as well as running the B&B and holding down a full-time job, had a two-year-old son and was seven months pregnant with her second and withal was full of life and energy. We had asked for a light evening meal, which as interpreted by Eleri turned out to be fresh melon followed by a huge salad of ham and every kind of vegetable with a wicked hazelnut gateau to finish.

Breakfast - yogurt and poached egg for me, the usual full Welsh for Dick - was early so that Eleri could go off to work, so we too had an early getaway. We set off for Llanboidy, only four miles or so, but it seemed to take a long time, with a sharp descent and another long hill to climb. With eyes on the verges, I noticed hart's tongue ferns and aquilegia. Llanboidy was like a French mountain village, with coloured houses of varying shapes and sizes climbing the hillside, and a municipal camping site in the centre of the village. This was the largest place we'd encountered since Carmarthen, having shop, post office and pub, and even boasting a bus service.

At Login we crossed the Taf, a river after which every Welshman is named and with yet more black arrows on the map we were relieved to reach at the top of the hill an adventure playground, again providentially supplied with seats, just at lunch time. The road was a single track one with passing places, so sometime in the afternoon we were amazed to meet not one but six school buses, each taking up the whole width of the road and leaving no room for even pedestrian traffic. Fortunately there were ditches to dive into. Surely, we thought, they must have been collecting the schoolchildren of the whole of Carmarthenshire.

At Llantissilio we were forced to walk along the A478 road coming from Cardigan, the first main road since Carmarthen. The traffic was heavy and unrelenting and kept us cowering in the verges. We had the consolation of finding a bakery with Welsh cakes, little fruity pancakes which were my 'find' among the local produce of South Wales.

Our destination for tonight was Nantyffin, a motel just along the road, the only place in the area to be doing B&B. This was unlike the present-day travel lodge, where the rooms are usually functional, providing shelter for the maximum number of travellers in the smallest possible space.

Nantyffin is a large place, set in an area of grassland and trees, having a lavishly appointed functions room as well as restaurant and bar. Our room too was large, with a separate bathroom and adjacent to its own covered space for our non-existent car. The scale on which the motel was built made me suspect that it dated from pre-war days, when people would go out motoring just for the fun of it. I imagined young men (usually men in those days) in leather coats driving open Bentleys with leather straps across the bonnet and women clad in flowing dustcoats and wearing hats with protective veils. Those were days of innocence, before we realised that there was a price to be paid for the freedoms bestowed by the motor car.

Nantyffin was under new management and being redecorated and that night we were the only guests, it being mid-week and out of season, so we felt rather marooned in the large restaurant. But the food was good, and Dick was treated to tasters of the three different kinds of draught beer on offer, a privilege which he rather regretted next morning.

The red sky at sunset had been deceptive, and we awoke to steady rain, which showed no sign of easing as we set out. The immediate event was crossing the Eastern Cleddau river, for once not at the foot of a steep hill, but more importantly marking the boundary between Camarthenshire and Pembrokeshire. There was now only one river of any size, the Western Cleddau, between us and St David's, and the black arrows were becoming less frequent.

Today we were making for Spittal, the one-time site of a hospital on a pilgrim's route from Llanfihangel on the South Wales coast which crossed the river there. Here we would reach the Pembroke peninsula called Dewiland after St David, and would cross it to reach the little cathedral city.

It was not a day to linger, cold as well as wet, and we were at Lower Haythog shortly after four in the afternoon. Lower Haythog is a farm guesthouse of the upmarket kind, and had

Eastern Cleddau to St David's

- Eastern Cleddau Rises
- Lower Haythog
- Spittal
- DYFED
- Western Cleddau Rises
- A 40
- Camrose
- Roch
- A 487
- Roch Gate
- St David's Head
- ST BRIDE'S BAY

a full complement of guests, none of them on foot. Our wet boots were rather frowned upon, and we were consigned to a small annexe outside the main building, perfectly adequate but rather cold until the heating came on. More seriously, there was no prospect of an evening meal, and since it was raining harder than ever there was no incentive to go out, so we supped on bread and cheese and went hungry to bed.

By morning it had already been raining for more than twenty-four hours and showed no immediate sign of stopping. Guests at breakfast were talking of visiting a cheese farm and a chocolate factory and exclaiming with wonder at my disclosure that I had walked across two countries. We'd by now become so accustomed to walking in the wet that the weather scarcely merited a mention. So we just replaced waterproofs and plodded on resignedly to meet and cross the A40 coming from Haverford West and aiming for its terminus at the ferry at Fishguard. This was the last we were to see of the A40 until our journey home.

We crossed the Western Cleddau by a tiny bridge with the waters seeming inadequate to make any impact on the large estuary it would soon join. In Camrose there were pub, post office and church all marked on our map; all were firmly shut, it seemed permanently, even the church which, with its white weathercock, is dedicated to St Ishmael.

One Giraldus, who in the twelfth century rode around Wales with his mentor Baldwin Archbishop of Canterbury in a recruitment drive for the Third Crusade, came through Camrose from Haverford West on the way to St David's. Edward Thomas suggests that Giraldus might have followed an 'ancient road of the same character as the Icknield Way' on his journey, but it seems most likely that the route would have been along the Tywi valley, now occupied by the A40, through St Clear and Whitland. Giraldus was born in Manorbier in Pembrokeshire and some believe that he is buried at St David's.

The lanes were full of purple foxgloves in their hundreds, making the verges shout on even this dull day. First cow parsley, then buttercups, now foxgloves all seemed to have had a bumper year. Foxgloves I know are biennials, having a two-year cycle of seed, germinate and bloom, but cow parsley and buttercups being perennials just seemed to have taken it on to spend themselves extravagantly for this one year.

The rain eased off and stopped, to be succeeded by a bank of sea-mist, a white roll of cotton wool advancing inexorably towards us. It was eerie and dreamlike to be so enveloped, as if one's sensation of moving had been lost, so there was no impression of distance being covered. When we unexpectedly met a couple of walkers, it was as if they had materialised from nowhere or been beamed down from another planet. Eventually the way started to descend and objects appeared out of the murk; it was of course and as usual past lunchtime, and we made a beeline for the church which had an outside seat.

No sooner had we settled ourselves than the rain came on with renewed vigour, as if to make up for the temporary lull and we hastily retreated to the shelter of the church lychgate, which didn't have a seat. After a while we tired of the immediate surroundings and of being cold and made a dash for it, down the hill and into Roch village, where the Spar grocer's was open, and across the road was our destination, Roch Gate motel.

Roch is another pilgrim village, possibly the last stop on the pilgrim route from the south, St David's being about ten miles distant along the coast road. The motel was the same kind of building as Nantyffin and boasted a leisure centre into the bargain. We booked in and repeated yesterday's routine of drying out and warming up before going across the road to the fish and chip shop. Our room looked out on to thorn bushes and grassland suggesting that somewhere below was the beach, but the seafog had returned, and with it our sense of isolation.

At this point we were not more than two miles from the sea at Newgale, but the next day we would be turning away from the coast to strike across the peninsula to St David's. 'Yippee,' I wrote in my diary. It looked as though I would be at St David's Head a day in advance of the summer solstice, which I had earlier chosen as my target for reaching the end of the walk. The summer solstice is regarded as an important Druidic date, so seemed appropriate in a land which is so closely associated with ancient religions.

We retraced our steps on to the plateau, passing Roch Castle which was spectacularly high on a hill-top, but had been quite invisible in the previous day's murk. It was a fine morning, the mist clearing to blue skies and warmth. This was perfect down-like country, with everywhere flowers that I associated with the seaside: thrift, harebells, scabious. We'd left the Preselli mountains somewhere behind, but ahead were odd-shaped spiky hills which I recognised as the Ordovician volcanic stumps rising above St David's Head.

Soon we had a glimpse of the sea, my first since Norfolk; when, just nine weeks ago I had looked back on it from the top of the hill above Thornham.

Our route made a wide dogleg north-east then west, there being a major obstruction for a direct approach to St David's in the shape of Brawdy airfield. The countryside seemed deserted, with widely dispersed farms, and a minute village or two. No sign of shop or pub, of course. At Llandeloy Dick asked at a house for water, and learned that shop and post-office had closed only six months previously. There was one bus a week going to Solva, the nearest small town, which couldn't be more than five miles distant.

We came to Middle Mill, where there was another steep river crossing - surely the last before St David's - and a woollen mill with a car park and a flurry of visitors. Reaching high ground again, we glimpsed a church spire in the distance, beyond yet another airfield. We avoided the busy coast road now within earshot and found a rough track and a ford to arrive in the main street of St David's as six o'clock was striking. There were ugly building works on the outskirts, but the centre of town was as I remembered it and unchanged and it felt like a homecoming. We hadn't booked any accommodation, and there were 'No vacancies' signs outside the first B&Bs we passed, but at the Crown we were directed around the corner to the Glyndwr Guest House in Nun Street. Nun is probably a corruption of Non, who was the mother of St David.

St David's is the smallest city in Great Britain, and is a renowned place of pilgrimage. St David was a native Welshman who lived in the sixth century and was a missionary and founder of monasteries in Wale. Miracles surround the story of his life, and from the eleventh century onward his shrine became the focus of pilgrimage for people of all ranks, including royalty, notably Henry II. Two pilgrimages to St David's were said to account for one to Rome. The cathedral itself dates from the twelfth century, but behind it the site of a monastic community is marked by St David's shrine. The cathedral, remarkable in its size and beauty, is set among fields hidden away in a hollow below the streets, with no dwellings near at hand to mar its impact, and the view from the lane above the cathedral is celebrated.

St David's has a lively atmosphere with little of the solemnity associated with holy places. The town has not been deserted by its youth as have so many small communities, and young people were clustered around the war memorial in the town centre, which seemed to be an agreed meeting place.

Yesterday's sunshine had marked only a brief respite in this June which meteorologists were to single out as being one of the coldest and wettest 'on record'. It was already starting to rain next morning as we set off for St David's Head, leaving our rucksacks at Glyndwr House to be collected later.

Past the cathedral and now roofless Bishop's Palace, we followed the motor road the two miles to its finish at White Sand Bay, and here at last found a gate and the white acorn waymark of the Pembrokeshire coast path. Unless you want to risk your neck by landing from the sea, the walker's route is the only feasible one to St David's Head, as it has been from Neolithic times. The whole countryside on the peninsula bears evidence of the settlement of this remote area by prehistoric peoples.

The Pembrokeshire coast path is yet another national trail reaching for nearly two hundred miles from St Dogmaels in the north to Amroth beyond Tenby on the South Wales coast. Most of the way the path goes over clifftops with many changes of gradient taking the path down to sea-level at times, and the walking is often rough and sometimes exposed. St David's Head is on National Trust property and is much visited for its wild scenery and comparative accessibility - it is less than two miles distant from the road at White Sand Bay.

It was only on reaching the coast path that it struck me that I was about to complete my side-to-side walk, and I turned to Dick and said with an air of surprise, 'Last lap'.

The walk was straightforward enough, climbing above the bay to a viewpoint above a small cove, the path hugging the cliff edge throughout, with its verges a mass of flowers and the cries of seabirds and sound of the incoming tide an ever-present accompaniment. St David's Head came into view, backed by the volcanic stumps Penbiri and Carn Lidi.

I had thought that the walk might be lacking a sufficiently dramatic climax, but not a bit of it! We crossed a small stream and climbed again to the cliff edge, turning a final exposed corner just as a squall drove in from the sea, bringing with it a fierce wind; for a while the seascape was blotted out. Buffeted by the wind I reached St David's Head in an undignified fashion on all fours, and sat on a rock to be photographed, not trusting myself to stand upright.

I might have believed that the squall had been put on for my benefit. By the time we had descended to shelter the worst was over and there was a gleam of sun. We sat on the clifftop and watched the peacefully ebbing tide, reluctant to leave and knowing that we had only the short walk to St David's and then would be taking whatever transport we could get to take us back to Llangadog. I felt the sadness which is an inevitable counterpoint to the joy of completing a long walk, knowing that this particular experience is unlikely to be repeated.

At White Sand Bay the car park was busy and people were taking surfboards down to the water. In less than an hour we were recovering our rucksacks and on our way east. After the general dearth of public transport in the back country I was surprised to discover there was an hourly bus service along the spectacular coast road to Haverford West, where we were deposited at the station - in the height of a thunderstorm no less. With great economy of resources the stations of Welsh Trains are unstaffed and lacking information about train times or destinations, but we found the crews of the occasional train more ready to tell us where they were going.

More by luck than good judgement we managed to board, first the train to Llanelli, then a smaller one crowded with noisy young people returning to their villages after a day out in Swansea. It was a shock to find ourselves leaving the train at Llandovery station in the early evening only four hours after setting out from St David's. Having decided to pick up the car from Cynyll in the morning, we booked in for the night at the Castle Hotel, finding that George Borrow had slept here; he seems to have occupied as many beds as Queen Elizabeth I.

For nearly all the way to Oxford next day we drove along the A40, of which I was beginning to feel quite fond. At least it was taking traffic away from those little roads of South Wales.

And there must be a moral there somewhere!

Chapter 13

For the Record

> We walk for a thousand reasons.
> Edward Thomas.

So I completed my side-to-side walk, on June 20th, a day ahead of schedule. I walked in total some four hundred and sixty miles, and took public transport for a few more, probably not more than twenty. The walk was done over a period of nine weeks, which included ten 'off' or rest days. (I have found that many people ask me for the above statistics, although in practice they seem unimportant.)

Maps aren't entirely to be relied upon when working out distances, because a two-dimensional spread can't take account of the third dimension of height, but I find a good rough estimate can be obtained by counting kilometre grid squares between points. Another good measure is time taken over distance. There's Naismith's rule which says that you calculate on walking at three miles an hour, then add on a half hour for every thousand feet of ascent. I don't think such rules are too helpful for me because they don't include time taken for rests, route-finding and the like. So I estimate an average of two miles an hour counting halts, and on this walk this usually resulted in six-hour days, occasionally more. On that, I don't think I walked more than fifteen miles on any day, and my overall average was about ten miles.

I ended the walk fitter than when I started, having lost six pounds in weight and well weather-beaten. I can't say suntanned because there wasn't too much sun in the latter stages. Having started out with creaky knees, I found that by ignoring it the pain went away, and I had little in the way of aches and pains - the ordinary end-of-day fatigue ceases to count after a time. I didn't have a single blister.

I wore my ageing Brasher boots throughout and they still serve me well for walks around South London although now down-at-heel, which isn't bad considering that they cost me only £25 in 1991. I must let the makers K boots know. In the wet weather of the final two weeks my Goretex jacket resolutely kept out the wet and as Goretex aficionados will know, was a great windshield. Otherwise, I was wearing the clothes I normally wear for any country walk.

I had a daily budget of thirty pounds for food, bed and breakfast, which usually worked out.

My return to earth was relatively painless; the squirrels this year had not found the strawberry crop, which was an abundant one and needed seeing to. I kept meeting people who didn't know I'd been away, and soon it felt like that, except for the pile of photographs and logbooks and other bits of memorabilia which sat on my desk waiting for me to be ready to attend to them. Which is what I'm doing now.

I've never felt comfortable in answering the question, 'Did you enjoy it?' especially as applied to a long distance walk. There are times when self-evidently one isn't enjoying it, and this was true about my walk across the home counties. I was depressed to find the extent of the changes which had taken place even since I walked from Beachy Head to Cape Wrath, and where it was becoming increasingly difficult to escape from traffic. I was left with the feeling that the few open spaces which were left were becoming so encroached upon that they would end up as isolated enclaves rather like the reservations built for American Indians in the United States, and that people like me who fled the crowds would be caged in like the animals in a safari park.

Because I was walking through the heavily populated south-east these changes were brought into sharp focus. I found it hard to accept that what is now described as the car economy and its consequences is taken for granted by generations reared since the end of world war two. The near-universal use of the motor car has produced car parks, new roads, garish motorway cafes, housing developments, noise, pollution, litter, fly-tipping, supermarkets, caravan sites, incessant traffic, even gridlock in towns and cities. Hardest of all was the realisation that there is no going back to an age when all these things didn't exist; we have to treat them as part of modern living and try as best we can to protect the environment against their worst effects.

So why do it at all, you may ask - a question I have asked myself many times. Looking for the answer is like taking skins off an onion - there's always another layer underneath. To say it's for the sheer pleasure of walking is just the outer layer, although I do believe that being on foot is the very best way of travelling wherever one happens to be. There is no other way of really seeing one's country, the bad as well as the good. Too easily, the eye skates over what it doesn't want to see and misses the good things when they can be left behind between one motorway junction and the next. It is only by walking that the landscape can be known in all its intimate detail, in the way that our far-off ancestors must have known it as they trod the ancient ways on foot because there was no other means of travel.

The scale on which our countries - England, Wales, Scotland and Ireland - are built means that the countryside is supremely accessible. There is the story of how an Alpine guide brought to the foot of Snowdon asked how many days it would take to reach the summit. He was comparing it to Mont Blanc, the highest mountain in Europe, which needs usually two overnight stages. A reasonably fit walker can stand on the summit of Snowdon within three hours of leaving Llanberis. There are few open spaces which cannot be reached on foot, and when new 'freedom to roam' legislation is enacted, we shall have access to many more acres of open land as well as the thousands of miles of footpaths available to us now.

We as humans, sadly, pollute the earth wherever we go, but of all methods of getting about, walking is the least damaging to our environment, and I believe this is true even where areas are over-visited and over-walked. The scars left by feet heal in time, whereas those created by bulldozers and quarries are near enough permanent.

But once all the layers have been peeled off, at the heart of the onion must lie a need. Perhaps it is the same need as the one felt by those first walkers when, their survival instincts satisfied, they started to make the same tracks along which I had walked. Perhaps we all have a gene which expresses that need. 'Go and look behind the ranges' wrote Kipling; 'We shall not cease from exploration' declared Eliot. In the world today there are few enough new places to explore; modern communications and transport have seen to that. So everybody has to find his or her own way to satisfy the need. Going off on a solo walk was my way of doing it. It's my way of creating space for myself, about seizing time out of life which is for me alone. It's a personal way of spring cleaning, where the cluttered chambers of my mind are swept bare.

I started out with all sorts of worries about my health, my fitness, my age - whether there was any point in going at all. I came back feeling that none of these things mattered; that I had learned more about myself and the country I live in. In place of the clutter were memories of the moments when magically and unexpectedly I was able to make sense of what I was doing. Faintly-drawn horizons which moved as I approached them; a rocking chair looking out on a walled garden; sleeping sheep on a Welsh hillside; serried ranks of foxgloves in a wet lane - more than enough to fill the chambers of memory.

My friend Lesley said some chapters ago that it's becoming harder to escape from traffic noise, which I take as a metaphor for our times. But I shall continue to be optimistic that it is possible that the earth in general and our countryside in particular is tough enough to withstand and can in the end recover from the abuse being flung at it.

I went back to Norfolk in late February for an away weekend. With our good friends Sandra and John, Dick and I stayed again at Orchard House in Thornham where I had been the previous April. It was clear and cold and windy and we filled our lungs with clean sea air. We walked along bits of the coast path which I had missed out, and saw the henge at Holme-next-the Sea - the ancient wooden circle which had in past months been uncovered by the tides after being entombed in peat for four thousand years. We watched the flocks of birds coming in to roost and preparing to start their long flight north for the summer, and observed the care which was being taken to protect them and the countryside and coast around them. The woods were full of snowdrops. The weekend in a small way reinforced my optimism and made me feel very fortunate.

For the future, well, I'm not sure how long the next walk will be, but I have this feeling that there's more to learn about ancient roads. I have yet to finish the Ridgeway, and from Overton Hill there's a Wessex Ridgeway which continues along the chalk ridge which started in Norfolk and ends at Lyme Regis.........Millennium year might be a good time to go.

A selected Bibliography.

Blatchford B. *Long Distance Walker's Handbook* A&C Black
Borrow George. *Wild Wales*
Cox R H. *The Green Roads of England* Garnstone 1914 (and reprints)
Curtis N. *The Ridgeway* Countryside Commission Guide 1994
Icknield Way Association. *A Guide to the Icknield Way Path*
Jones J. *Offa's Dyke Path* HMSO 1976
Marriott M. *The footpaths of Britain* Queen Anne Press 1984
Robinson. *Peddar's Way and North Norfolk Coast Path Guide* HMSO
Thomas, Edward. *The Icknield Way* Constable 1916
Toulson S. *The Giraldus Journey* Michael Joseph 1988

INDEX

A40, 13, 95, 121, 127, 131,
  135, 145, 157, 164
Accidents, 38-9
Afon Cothi, 142-3
Age and ageing, 55-6
Akeman Street, 103

Backpack, contents of, 15-16
Balsham, 61-2
Barnham, 46
Bayliss, Mrs, 102
Beavons, Anne, 124
Bed and breakfast, 26-7, 46, 62
  Balsham, 62
  Bledlow, 79-80
  Buscot, 98
  Capel Isaac, 142
  Castle Acre, 37-9
  Checklist, 152-3
  Cinderford, 117
  Coln St Alwyns, 102
  Dunstable, 73
  Great Chesterford, 64-5
  Great Trehiw, 123-4
  Lack of, 44, 51, 81, 116, 119,
    132, 137
  Llandovery, 135
  Minsterworth, 115-16
  Monmouth, 121-2
  North Pickenham, 40-1
  Sheringham, 21
  Stetchworth, 56-7
  Thornham, 28

Wendover, 77
Betterton, Sandra and John, 66
Bird watching, 27, 51
Bisley, 108
Black Mountains, 123, 125, 126
Blakeney, 23
Bledlow, 78, 79
Boudicca, 31
Brancaster, 28
Brecon Beacons, 131
Brinkley, 60
Burnham Deepdale, 27-8
Burnham Overy Staithe, 26
Bury St Edmunds, 53
Buscot, 98

Carmarthen, 145
Carter, Mrs, 116
Castle Acre, 37-9
Cavenham Nature Reserve, 51
Cheating, 24-5
Chevely, 55
Cinderford, 117
Cirencester, 104-5
  Park, 105-6
Cley, 23
Coke, Thomas, 26
Coleford, 118-19
Countryside Alliance, 146-7
Crickhowell, 126-7
Cromer, 14
Crowmarsh Gifford, 82
Cycling, 55, 108

171

Cynyll Farm, 136-7

Davies, Anne, 125-6
Deacon Hill, 72
Dunn, Lesley, 43, 49, 52, 54
Dunstable, 59, 73-4

Eastleach Turville, 100

Flowers, 16, 22, 28, 33, 49, 54, 62, 76, 97, 116, 119, 126, 153, 158
Food, 29, 62 *see also* Pubs
Footpaths, 32, 80, 97
  see also under individual paths
Forest of Dean, 117-18

Geoff and Gill, 106-7
Giles, Tim, 144
Giraldus, 157-8
Gloucester, 113
Gonzooglers, 127, 128
Goring-on-Thames, 84-5
Grand Union Canal, 76
Great Bircham, 33-4
Great Chesterford, 64
Greenway, Mrs, 62
Grim's Ditch, 82, 84
Guidebooks, 15-16, 24, 34, 46
Guinness, Val, 37-9

Halfway (village), 134
Hengrave, 50
Herringswell, 53
Hill farmers, 147-8

Hillaby, John, 14
Hitchin, 59
Holkham Hall, 26
Holme-next-the-Sea, 170
Home counties, 83
Houghton Hall, 35

Ickleford, 67-8, 71-5
Icknield Way, 12, 46-7, 52-3, 59, 62

Jacuzzis, 153
Joyce's Cross, 109

Kennett, 53
King, Mrs, 64-5
Kymin, The, 121, 122

Lady Anne's Drive, Norfolk, 26
Lea Valley Walk, 72
Letchworth, 59, 67
Linton, 63
Little Massingham, 36
Llanboidy, 153-4
Llandovery, 135, 137
Llantony, 126
Llanvihangel Crucorny, 125
Lloyd, Haydn and Eleri, 152-3
Loneliness, 23, 25, 44, 65, 68
Losing things, 24, 34-5
Lower Haythog, 155-7
Lowestoft, 14

Maps, 15-16, 27, 50, 51-2, 108, 140 *see also* Guidebooks
Military presence in rural areas,

42, 43, 53
Monks Risborough, 77
Monmouth, 121-2
Monmouthshire & Brecon
    canal, 128
Muckleburgh Museum, 22

Nantyffin motel, 154-5
Norfolk coast path, 19
Norris, Mr, 40-1
North Pickenham, 40-1

Obstacles, 17
Offa's Dyke, 122, 123
Oilseed rape, 60, 61, 63, 72

Painswick, 109
Pant Gwyn, 144
Peddar's Way, 31-3, 36-7, 40, 41-3
Pembrokeshire coast path, 161-2
Pencelli, 129
Pennine Way, 9-10
Planning, 10, 11
Pockthorpe Corner, 42
Preseli mountains, 152
Princes Risborough, 78
Pubs, 26, 28, 50, 51, 54, 56, 60, 90, 103

Reay, Mrs, 98
Red kites, 123, 141, 142
Reed Herbert, Mrs, 56-7
Rest days, 68-9, 137
Ridgeway, 75-6, 80-1, 86-91

Ridgeway Lodge, 89-91
Rights of way, 97, 140-1
    see also Footpaths
Roads, 12, 39, 78
    see also A40
Roch, 159
Royston, 59, 66
Rucksack, 16
    see also Backpack
RUPPs, 80

St David's, 160-2
St David's Head, 162-3
Sally, 85-93
Salthouse, 23
Sapperton, 107
Scutchamer Knob, 91
Sedgeford, 33
Segsbury Down, 91-2
Severn river, 95, 113, 117
Sheep, 124
Sheringham, 21-2
Skirrid, 123
Smith, Ann, 27
Smith, Mr (Wallingford), 81, 82-3
Smith, Mr and Mrs (Capel Isaac), 142
Sponsored events, 39, 55, 92
Stiffkey, 24
Stiles, 41
Stonebridge, 43
Summer solstice, 159
Supermarkets, 19, 55, 78

Thames path, 84
Thetford, 44-5
Thomas, Edward, 13, 143, 149, 157, 165
The Icknield Way, 11-12
Thornham, 28-9, 169
Tombs family history, 99, 100-102
Tombs, Dick, 14, 15, 18, 29, 35-7, 59, 94, 104, 121, 136-62
Tombs, Joyce
  By Way of Beachy Head, 8, 10, 91, 109
  and Wales, 111-13
  see also Joyce's Cross
Traffic, 17, 78, 167, 169
Trains, 22, 53, 77-8, 85, 163
Trecastle, 133

Trebersed Farm, 145-6
Tuddenham, 52-3

Village names, 40

Wallingford, 81, 82, 83
Weather, 17, 37, 40, 54, 112, 133-4, 142-4, 158
Wells-next-the-Sea, 25
Wendover, 77
Weybourne, 22
White Horse Hill (Uffington), 93-4
Woolstone, 94

By the same Author:

BY WAY OF BEACHY HEAD

In 1991 and 1992, Joyce walked from Beachy Head on the Sussex coast to Cape Wrath on the northernmost point of Scotland. The diaries she made at the time developed into her first book, published in 1996.

By Way of Beachy Head has been widely acclaimed. The *Daily Telegraph* summed it up - "Simple, uplifting and worth a hundred Ffiona Campbells". Walking and rambling magazines gave it generous coverage, and featured Joyce as a walker to be taken seriously.

Copies are available, price £6.00, from bookshops or direct from the publisher.